THE HOLOCAUST BY BULLETS

Published with the support of the United States Holocaust Memorial Museum

THE HOLOCAUST BY BULLETS

A Priest's Journey to
Uncover the Truth behind the
Murder of 1.5 Million Jews

FATHER PATRICK DESBOIS

with a foreword by Paul A. Shapiro

palgrave
macmillan

THE HOLOCAUST BY BULLETS
Copyright © Father Patrick Desbois, 2008.
English language translation © Catherine Spencer, 2008 All rights reserved.
First published in English in 2008 by PALGRAVE MACMILLAN® in
the US–a division of St. Martin's Press LLC, 175 Fifth Avenue, New York,
NY 10010.

Where this book is distributed in the UK, Europe and the rest of the world,
this is by Palgrave Macmillan, a division of Macmillan Publishers Limited,
registered in England, company number 785998, of Houndmills, Basingstoke,
Hampshire RG21 6XS.

Palgrave Macmillan is the global academic imprint of the above companies
and has companies and representatives throughout the world.

Palgrave® and Macmillan® are registered trademarks in the United States,
the United Kingdom, Europe and other countries.

**Published with the support of the United States Holocaust
Memorial Museum**

ISBN-13: 978-0-230-60617-3
ISBN-10: 0-230-60617-2

Desbois, Patrick.
    [Porteur de mémoires. English]
    The Holocaust by bullets : a priest's journey to uncover the truth behind
the murder of 1.5 million Jews / by Patrick Desbois.
        p.   cm.
    ISBN 0-230-60617-2
    1. Jews—Persecutions—Ukraine.   2. Holocaust, Jewish (1939–1945)—
Ukraine—Personal narratives.   3. Ukraine—Ethnic relations.   4.
Desbois, Patrick.   I. Title.
DS135.U4D4813   2008
940.53'1809477—dc22

                                                        2008002472

A catalogue record of the book is available from the British Library.

*The translation of this work received financial support from the French Ministry of
Foreign Affairs, the Cultural Services of the French Embassy in the United States and
FACE (French American Cultural Exchange).*

*French Voices Logo
designed by Serge
Bloch*

Design by Letra Libre

First edition: August 2008
10   9   8   7   6   5   4   3   2   1
Printed in the United States of America.

CONTENTS

Photosection appears between pages 120 *and* 121.

FOREWORD

Before German bureaucrats met in early 1942 at Wannsee outside Berlin to elaborate plans for the deportation and mechanized murder of European Jewry in extermination camps. Before the Birkenau killing center opened near Auschwitz. Before Treblinka, Sobibor, Belzec, or Majdanek assumed their full fury. Before all of this, hundreds of thousands of Jews from a number that would grow quickly to over 1.5 million had already been murdered by the Germans, their Axis allies and local collaborators in the towns and villages of Ukraine, Belarus, Russia, and other republics of the USSR.

These first mass victims of the Holocaust were not transported in crowded cattle cars to secluded sites far from their homes, removed from the consciousness of anyone who might have known them as neighbor, schoolmate, client or friend, or who might still acknowledge their humanity. Nor were they murdered in the industrialized killing centers the Nazis built in Poland, with their high barbed wire fences, gas chambers, and crematoria that define "Holocaust" for most of us.

These victims—mostly women, children, and old people—were taken from their homes, on foot or by cart or truck, to locations just outside the towns and villages where they lived, if even that far. There they were shot, usually the same day or hour, at close range, face to face or in the back, one human being killing another, and all in the presence of local residents, the victims' non-Jewish neighbors, even friends. The murders were coordinated by German special killing squads—the *Einsatzkommandos*—but the shooters included German SS, *Wehrmacht* troops, Romanian military, and special "operational squadrons" (*esaloane operative*), order police units from the surrounding area, as well as special SS units formed of willing local nationals or *Volksdeutsch* volunteers. The killing sites now are all but invisible. They offer up none of the architectural design elements that shape the iconic imagery of Holocaust memorial sites worldwide—"*Arbeit Macht Frei*" encased in ironwork, the curve of the arched gateway to Auschwitz-Birkenau, or the chimney of a crematorium. There is no architecture of destruction here. Even the place names—Bogdanivka (where more Jews were murdered than at Babi Yar), Busk, Novozlatopol, Torchyn, Bielogorsk, Voskresenske, and hundreds of others—fail to register or resonate with most students of the Shoah.

These first mass victims of the Holocaust went largely forgotten through most of the post–World War II era. Their stories and the fates of their communities were obscured by clouds of Soviet secrecy and anti-Semitism. While we slowly but surely came to understand the detailed operation of the Nazi concentration camp system in the west, Soviet totalitarianism restricted our knowledge about the east. Access to Holocaust-related documentary materials that might have fallen into Soviet hands or been created by Soviet authorities was denied. Interviewing people who could give eyewitness testimony was virtually impossible and likely to create difficulties for willing interviewees. Even access to the localities where the murders took place, if one could identify them, was restricted. Focus on the Jewish specificity of the Holocaust was taboo. The names of the victims, revealed by their Jewishness, the towns and villages where they lived and died, and the locations of the mass graves where they lay remained unknown and unmarked.

This was just as the Nazis and their collaborators had wanted. Their goal had been to make it as if those first hundreds of thousands, then millions of innocent Jewish victims had never existed.

The situation began to change with *Perestroika* and the demise of the Soviet Union, when it became possible to access Soviet archives. But that was not sufficient. Only today, thanks to a cooperative effort inspired by Father Patrick Desbois and the Yahad-In Unum Association, supported by the Catholic Church of France,[1] and involving the United States Holocaust Memorial Museum in Washington, the *Fondation pour la Memoire de la Shoah* and *Memorial de la Shoah* in Paris, and some others, can we detect dramatic progress. We are succeeding finally in lifting the veil that has clouded understanding of what happened on the ground in the east and obscured our memory of those who fell victim to the Holocaust in the half of the European continent where Jews were murdered brutally, individually, and often publicly, near their homes, shot into pits or in open fields, sometimes buried alive, sometimes within the sight of children.

After the disintegration of the U.S.S.R., the United States Holocaust Memorial Museum undertook an intensive effort to microfilm Holocaust-related documents in archival repositories of the newly independent former Soviet republics. The collections were much more voluminous than anticipated, including, for example, the records of the "Extraordinary State Commission to Investigate German-Fascist Crimes Committed on Soviet Territory" (USHMM Archives Record Group 22.002M) and massive collections of war crimes trials relating to the Holocaust from former KGB archives (USHMM Archives Record Group RG31.018M, for example, covers Ukrainian trials). Soviet authorities had been anxious to document atrocities and identify and try

German perpetrators and local collaborators. No country was as stead-
fast in pursuing retribution against the killers. The result was a wealth
of documentary material full of detailed information—lists of names of
victims, testimonies of eyewitnesses, signed depositions, pretrial investigations, protocols of interrogations, indictments, court proceedings,
diagrams—well over five million pages collected thus far, with more
still to come.[2]

And yet, despite the availability of this rich material, it was little
used. Language was a problem, and many hand-written documents
were difficult to decipher even for researchers with well-honed language skills. More critically, the reliability of the documentation was a
concern. The Soviet regime had misrepresented the truth on so many
occasions that many people, including field-leading scholars, questioned the veracity of the documents. The murder of the Jews was
often characterized in these files as the killing of "heroic Soviet resistance fighters" rather than the genocidal extermination of a people.
How reliable could the documents be if even this fundamental truth
was denied? And with so many show trials in the Soviet past, could one
believe evidence brought forward in postwar trials of alleged collaborators, especially when many of them were *Volksdeutsch,* Ukrainians, Lat-
vians, or members of some other nationality whose loyalty was suspect
in Soviet eyes?

Thus the shroud that hung over what we knew of the first mass victims of the Holocaust remained, until the extraordinary work of Father
Desbois opened a way forward. Motivated by family history, ethical
fiber, faith, and fervor for remembrance, he has undertaken, as he de-
scribes in *The Holocaust by Bullets,* to locate the mass graves of the victims in Ukraine and to record videotaped testimony from hundreds of
eyewitnesses who have never spoken publicly before—people who in

their youth saw their Jewish neighbors, acquaintances, friends, even schoolmates and lovers murdered. These new testimonies are confirming much of the content of the Soviet documentation, and through corroboration of this source also enable us to give credence to information in the Soviet investigative reports that a youthful individual observer would have had no ability to know. Similarly, the Soviet investigation and trial records confirm that the individuals giving testimony to Father Desbois today are remembering accurately what they saw, despite the passage of more than 60 years. Further, the personal relationships with victims revealed in these new testimonies and the sheer emotional power of the act of remembrance provide insights and perspectives that would have had no place in official Soviet postwar reports. That the eyewitnesses remember should not be surprising. Most of them have lived in isolated locations, with little access to outside sources of information that might have seeped into and altered their memories. When one sees their taped testimonies, or reads the transcripts of their revelations, one knows that these eyewitnesses could not have forgotten what they saw. They were condemned to remember. Nevertheless, without the confirmation provided by the old Soviet records, the deniers, the relativizers, and the trivializers would one day have called their testimony, given so late, into question.

We can now know the whole truth in all of its frightening detail. Through a magical marriage of the evidence—60-year-old Soviet documentation and riveting testimonies taken today, to which Father Desbois has added astonishing ballistic and forensic findings as well—we are finally able to see clearly. The first 1.5 million victims of the Holocaust did not "disappear" from the face of the earth, or from human consciousness, as the Nazis had hoped. Father Desbois has found the mass graves where the victims lie. He is telling their stories and arranging for

Kaddish (Jewish prayer for the dead) to be recited in their memory . . . finally. He is demonstrating that even under the most difficult circumstances—travel to these locations is grueling, the mass grave sites often desecrated, confrontation with exposed human remains debilitating, and the testimony overwhelming even for a priest—the memory of victims who seemed nameless and unknowable can be recovered.

As Father Desbois navigates between archival study visits to Washington and the hundreds of now-adult/then-child eyewitnesses that are guiding him to mass grave sites in Ukraine, he is restoring to hundreds of thousands of victims too long forgotten the humanity that the Nazis sought to strip from them. The victims were not nameless corpses. By restoring their memory, he is resurrecting our own humanity as well and denying victory to the perpetrators and to all who have sympathized or may yet sympathize with them.

The Holocaust by Bullets project has memorial and testimonial significance beyond anything we have encountered for a long time. The mass grave sites strewn across Ukraine inspire horror, but require reverence. Most of the sites will never be located if not found now, while eyewitnesses to the killings can identify them. The pained faces of the eyewitnesses—nearly all Christian—as they reveal long-suppressed inner torment remind us of the danger of unchecked anti-Semitism, not only for Jews but for everyone. Father Desbois' work is already having an impact on Holocaust research and education in France and elsewhere.[3] And in the future the results of his work will help to combat Holocaust denial, in particular in Ukraine, Belarus, and other places where *The Holocaust by Bullets* has relevance and resonance that Auschwitz and the iconography of the Nazi death camps do not.

The bystanders' failure to act during the Holocaust empowered the perpetrators and contributed to the immensity of the loss. Father

Patrick Desbois, a man of profound personal faith, understands not only the necessity for prayer, but the power of words and teaching, and most of all the importance of action. Christianity calls for "acts of loving kindness" (*misericordia*) and Judaism for the *mitzvah* (good deed) of "*tikkun olam*" (healing the world). Father Desbois is fulfilling the strictures of both faiths, as readers of *The Holocaust by Bullets* will quickly recognize. In the process, he reminds us in powerful fashion of the shared heritage, shared interests, and shared vulnerability of these two great Abrahamic religious traditions. All of us—Christians and Jews, the victims whose memory he has retrieved and the eyewitnesses whose consciences he has relieved, Holocaust survivors and survivors of the other genocides, people of good will of all faiths and in all countries—owe him a debt of gratitude.

Paul A. Shapiro
Director, Center for Advanced Holocaust Studies
United States Holocaust Memorial Museum

Polina Pavlona Katsenko, Bassan, January 2, 2007

She is frail and slight in her red sweater and yellow headscarf. She is sitting at a table covered with a waxed tablecloth with flowers, and her little blue eyes sparkle with intelligence as she speaks: "When I was 14, I joined the Red Army as a nurse and accompanied the troops all the way to central Asia. The German fascists started to lose. Then my army corps entered Poland and went to Krakow. I found myself close to Auschwitz, a big camp that had been built to kill the Jews. I wrote a report that was read in the *kolkhozes:*[1]

"Where we come from the Nazis machine-gun the Jews but in the west they kill them in camps."

UKRAINE, SPRING 2007

March 31, 2007, 10 A.M.

Outside the window of our blue van the lush Ukrainian landscape streamed before my eyes. The first blooms had started to appear on the fruit trees. For the last two hours we had been driving in silence along a bumpy road in the region of Lutsk, not far from Belarus. The low-roofed houses were painted in amazing colors, canary yellow side by side with brick-red.

The wood fences along the sides of the road were also painted yellow. The farmers were busy in the fields with horses and carts, sowing or spreading compost on the plowed land. The brown, almost black earth revealed its richness in wide-open furrows. We saw very few tractors in this part of Volhynia and the rare cars we passed were all Ladas in various colors.

Mid-morning, we finally reached our destination: Senkivishvka, a small village with an orthodox church, a town hall, and one shop that has not changed since the Soviet era. The shop stocked a little of everything—in other words, nothing much: white bread, black bread, smoked herring and mackerel, very greasy bacon, a few tomatoes, three eggs, and a few toys. The shopkeeper, dressed in a traditional blue and white smock, weighed a piece of bacon and added up the total on an abacus. An old lady walked along the side of the road holding a bunch of plastic flowers in one hand. She was returning from the central market. We approached her and asked her if she lived here during World War II. After a brief discussion, she pointed out the house of the former school principal, Vassil, whom she said had a keen interest in local history. Outside Vassil's house an enormous black dog, fenced in by wire netting, seemed determined to break down the gate of his cage. The retired schoolmaster appeared at the door and welcomed us as if we were old friends. He took us to see Luba. Sixty-one years earlier, she and her sister Vira witnessed a murder they never could to forget, that of the village Jews.

One of the sisters still lived in the same house, in view of the mass grave. She was very moved when she saw us and sat down on a little blue wooden bench outside her house. Dogs were barking in the distance and geese paraded noisily about the place in groups of three or four. She told her story very simply, like the child she was at the time might have told it.

———————

She had seen the trucks drive past their house, not far away. Early that morning the farmers had been forced to dig an immense ditch, "over there" she says pointing with her left hand. Each truck unloaded 50 Jews from the village, mainly women and children. These people were her neighbors, friends, and classmates. She told us that in 1941 the village school included Poles, Ukrainians, and Jews.

At the edge of the ditch the earth had been packed into a makeshift ladder. The Jews undressed, while the guards beat them. Completely naked, family after family, fathers, mothers, and children went calmly down the steps and lay face down on top of the bodies of those who had just been shot. A man called Humpel, a German policeman, advanced, upright, walking on the dead bodies, pistol in hand, and murdered each Jew, one after the other, with a bullet in the back of the neck. Less than 10 meters away, the two sisters saw everything. Before starting his work that morning, Humpel had put on a white coat like a doctor's smock, and then had gone down into the ditch. Luba thinks he wanted to protect his uniform. At regular intervals, he stopped shooting, climbed out of the pit, took a break, drank a small glass of liquor, and went back into the ditch. Naked, another Jewish family climbed down into the ditch and lay face down. The massacre lasted one full day.

Humpel killed all the Jews in the village, single-handed.

Later I visited her sister Vira, who lives in another village. She confirmed Luba's statement. They were together, 61 years ago, living next to the mass grave. Vira adds that Humpel, the man who murdered the Jews, was killed by Bandera's[2] resistance fighters in the forest not far from her village.

After interviewing these two women I got back into the van. I had just recorded the testimony of the 460th witness to the murder of Jews in the Ukraine.

Originally from the Bresse area in the Saône-et-Loire region of France, I have been a Catholic priest for 20 years. That evening I took time to think. How had I, a French Catholic, ended up in Ukraine listening to old peasants describing their eyewitness experience in the so-called "Holocaust by bullets" in their villages?

I looked out of the window in silence. That day, I had seen a white horse and a brown horse harnessed together being led out to plow.

Women, their heads covered with multicolored scarves, carrying brushes and metal basins, walked to the village cemetery to clean the graves of their families before Easter. The daffodils and primroses were beginning to display their bright colors. Every landscape reminded me of my childhood. I had seen all these scenes before, a long time ago, elsewhere, in France. My grandparents, Victorine and Emile at Ville-gaudin in Bresse, also had two draft horses, a brown one that was very good-natured, and a grey one that bit. I loved driving them, sitting with my grandparents on the cart carrying the wood we had gathered in the forest. Our neighbors yoked their oxen together to pull hay or straw at the end of the summer. After each mass, my grandmother would go to each of the family graves to adjust a flowerpot knocked over by the wind, or to clean a monument stained by the rain, and to say a little prayer for the dead.

In Ukraine I quite often found myself thinking of all those who had carried me through life and the faith. Actions, sounds, and traditions that were handed down to me enabled me, in that atmosphere that I thought had disappeared, to listen to those men and women who are as simple as my family was and who do not want people to forget what happened.

How did the paths of my native Bresse countryside, of my child-hood, come to intersect today with those of the witnesses to the Nazi crimes and the murder of the Jewish people of Ukraine? That is what I shall try, as best I can, to relate.

I

ORIGINS

I spent my early childhood living with my paternal grandparents in Saint-Laurent, a neighborhood on the banks of the river in Chalon-sur-Saône that was not quite town and not quite the countryside. Claudius, my grandfather, was a farmer and a poultry provider for my parents' cheese and poultry shop. Every morning at dawn he set out on the roads leading to the villages of central Bresse in a little gray truck with empty wooden cages strapped to it. Every day he traveled to a different village, where the weekly market was held. People came to buy chickens, ducks, turkeys, pigeons, rabbits, eggs, and butter from the farmers. For me the days of the week corresponded to the names of the villages where the markets were held: Wednesday, Saint-Martin; Thursday, Saint-Germain-du-Plain; Friday, Mervans; and so on.

At nine in the morning, the town bell marking the opening of the market would ring over a market square that was already bustling with life. The chicken buyers, who had long been seated at an outdoor café, could finally rush toward the center of the market and the cages full of fowl. They had to be fast. From a very young age my grandfather taught me how to recognize good birds, and the tricks of negotiating for the best fowl in the Bresse region. At the end of the day I would stuff the squawking and flapping birds into the cages on our truck. The afternoons were spent in the plucking house where the birds and rabbits had to be killed and prepared for sale. I was my grandfather's "apprentice." Everybody said I looked like him.

Later, I lived with my parents who had a small shop in a narrow street in the middle of town, rue aux Fèvres, on the corner of the rue des Cloutiers. Eventually I discovered that this was in the old Jewish neighborhood of Chalon. The shop was called *Au bon gruyère* ("Home of the good gruyère"). As the name suggested, we sold cheese, mainly gruyère that we bought in 50-kilo rounds, but also the fowl that my grandfather bargained for in the villages. For the holidays, particularly Christmas, my uncles, aunts, and cousins came to help us pluck the chickens and prepare them. For us, Christmas meant the birth of Jesus but also a steady stream of customers coming to collect their turkeys.

My mother's family was called Rivière, like a river, my father's Dubois, like the woods. Some names lend a whole landscape to life, as did these. Life was simple and very lively, from school to the shop, from the shop to the slaughterhouse, from the slaughterhouse to the village farms, Chalon to Bresse. Every day we rode our bicycles steering our 13 cows to the meadows 10 kilometers from the house.

A sense of justice and a job well done were the twin pillars of my family. Being curious about life, I asked my parents to place a small chair, a little straw-bottomed affair, beside the shop door so that I could sit and watch the people on the sidewalk. The street and the passers-by were like a book that opened the world to me. My father always said: "The street is a theater!" Like the rest of my family, I knew all the people who lived on the street by name, regardless of their work, religion or nationality. My childhood friends were French, Italian, and Tunisian. It mattered little to me! My parents taught me a strict Catholic and humanistic ethic. My mother often repeated: "In the shop we must serve beggars in the same way we serve the Countess!" A countess did in fact come to the shop sometimes, in a blue convertible; she parked on the sidewalk and demanded: "A little piece of gruyere, please!" If there were other customers, my mother turned a deaf ear until her turn had come. Beggars also came to the shop with a meat voucher given to them by the municipality. My mother used to say to me: "You have to give them half a rabbit, but only give them the good bits, the thighs!" And we were perfectly happy to eat the rabbit ribs ourselves.

One part of my family was very Catholic, while another was athe-ist, even anticlerical. From childhood on, I knew I would have to make a choice about God and the Catholic Church. Some family dis-cussions resembled epic medieval debates, only a bit more friendly. There were always painful issues behind these disputes, which in-evitably ended with this question: "How could God exist and not react to the misery in the world?" Or sometimes: "Was Jesus's death on the cross the end of his story or had he really come back to life to play a role in the world?"

At the end of our little street stood the Cathedral of Saint Vincent which, seen through my child's eyes, seemed to be as large as the Cathe-dral of Notre Dame in Paris. I often went to mass alone because my parents worked on Sunday mornings. Two childhood experiences still live in my memory. The priest had said that Christ was really present at mass so, sitting on a wooden bench, I blinked my eyes as much as I could, especially when he burned incense, thinking: "I'm sure I will see

Him sooner or later!" Similarly, every year before Easter I listened attentively to the Holy Week readings. The priest said that every year "Jesus dies and rises from the dead." Every year I hoped it wouldn't happen. I used to think: "Maybe Jesus will be permitted to survive this year!" And every year, just before Easter, I was saddened to hear that He had been murdered again. Behind these two naïve memories lay the lessons my family had given me in simple words: believing in God and being aware of evil had to be expressed in prayers but also in actions, as a quest, and a responsibility toward others.

Every Sunday afternoon at the same time, after cleaning the shop, we closed the cream-colored folding shutters and set out for my maternal grandparents's house in the Bresse countryside. They lived in the farmhouse of the Chateau de la Marche, a castle that had been destroyed during the French Revolution.

Although I was born in 1955, 10 years after the end of World War II, the topography of my childhood was still heavily influenced by the geography of the war, with its divisions and violence. My grandfather Claudius lived about a hundred meters from a bridge where the line of demarcation passed, the famous line that separated France in two, the occupied zone to the north and the non-occupied or so-called "free" zone to the south. A little plaque had been placed on the bridge: "Line of demarcation." Each time we crossed the bridge, one of us shouted: "We've passed the demarcation line!" Our whole family life was immersed in war stories. I can still hear my mother, every Monday morning, perched on a step-ladder in order to reach the top of the shop window, washing the glass panes and singing at the top of her voice the refrains she must have heard from resistance fighters: "Flee, cowardly soldiers, you shall not pass!" From earliest childhood, I knew exactly who had collaborated with the Germans, which houses the Germans had burned down, and the places in the neighborhood where the men were taken to be shot.

My family always took the opportunity to give me a detailed account of the places where they had suddenly come face to face with history. They were simple people who wanted to tell us, the younger generations, what had happened, using places and traces where the war had marked our daily landscape. This was a human, ethical education in which people spoke little but where everything that happened became the material for a story or an epic. Very often I used to go up to the attic to see if the refugees had left something behind. I looked under the furniture and in the cupboards.

How often had I heard the story of the German plane shot down by the Communist resistance fighters! The plane fell into my maternal grandparents's fields. My mother's farm often provided fresh supplies to the resistance fighters, the *maquis,* and shelter to refugees from the east of France. German troops came to the farm to look for resistance fighters. Soldiers turned the house upside-down and threatened to shoot all the men in the household. I didn't find out until much later that the German pilots taken prisoner by the *maquis* had been tortured in my grandparents's farm before being shot in the forest across from the house. As an adult, it's strange to think that we used to play hide and seek in places where men were tortured. My mother only once said something on the subject: "They made me go outside when the Germans screamed too loudly because I was a little girl."

My maternal grandfather, Emile, who was a forest worker, often took me walking in the immense forests surrounding the farm. He spoke little and walked fast. He often pointed out certain trees which had what looked like scar marks on their barks: "See the impact of the bullets on these trees? See here, that's the trace left by a bullet when they shot a German." I was already learning that, for those who knew how to see and hear them, both nature and ordinary people bore the scars of history.

My maternal grandmother Victorine was in some ways the heroine of the family. One day I asked her if there had been any Jews among the refugees. She merely replied: "Why should I have asked them if they were Jewish?" I didn't really know what it meant to be a Jew. For me, the Jews were the Lévys who sold trousers on the square at Baune, and the Peres, our neighbors, who had come from Algeria. Faces, smiles, friends.

Another topography, strange, distant, and foreign, synonymous with misfortune and suffering, regularly appeared in the course of our family conversations. Other unknown names of distant towns and villages echoed through my life.

Mauthausen. A cousin had died there. He was a bus driver and crossed the demarcation line every day with his passengers. One evening he didn't come home. His wife could not get any information from the German authorities. Disappeared. A year later she received a letter, short and to the point. Her husband had died of pneumonia in Mauthausen.

Dachau. A cousin had come back from there. He lived with us. He had had tuberculosis since the war and no longer worked. He didn't speak much about his experiences in Dachau but went back there from time to time with other former deportees. He always returned sadder than when he left.

And then, there was one name, a name unlike all the others: *Rawa-Ruska.* I was told my grandfather Claudius had been taken there during the war. As usual, I tried to understand. I thought that if he didn't talk to me about it, it was because he must have done something bad. One day I asked him this terrible question: "Grandpa, did you kill any people?" Not even turning round to face me, he simply answered: "No." I didn't know how much the misery of deportation could isolate people, how much he must have thought that nobody in Chalon in 1970 could possibly understand what had happened in Rawa-Ruska back in 1942. I didn't know how sullied a person could feel after living through such horror.

And then one day, one summer morning, sitting beside him in the little gray truck, I pushed him, pushed him so much that he told me about his three escape attempts. I was seven years old.

He had tried to escape from the camp twice and failed, but on his third attempt his fellow-inmates helped him by stomping their clogs on the ground, making a racket to create a diversion while he jumped into a thicket. It was successful. He made it to the train station of Strasbourg, in Alsace, a region of France which had been annexed as part of Germany. He went to buy a ticket to return to his wife and son in Chalon-sur-Saône. He asked for a ticket in German. The lady behind the counter answered him in French. My grandfather paused for a moment: "In that instant I knew I had failed. She was going to report me! I didn't even make it to the train. The Gestapo arrested me. Destination Rawa-Ruska." Then my grandfather fell silent. And afterwards . . . ? There was no afterwards. This silence, from a man usually so cheerful, was charged with meaning. The silence had a name: *Rawa-Ruska.*

Several times during our Sunday lunches I tried to ask questions when he was absent. As soon as I pronounced the words Rawa-Ruska everybody started crying, especially Marie-Louise, my grandmother. Rawa-Ruska echoed like a painful family mystery. What a strange name! I didn't even know what country Rawa-Ruska was in. It was nowhere. It was impossible to situate it. Was it in Russia, Poland, or somewhere else? Just once, he uttered these words: "For us, the camp was difficult; there was nothing to eat, we had no water, we ate grass, dandelions. But it was worse for the others!" That sentence was engraved in my consciousness as a child for all time. I realized that he couldn't say any more about it. But who were the others?

I was 12 years old when I saw images of the Holocaust in the municipal library in Chalon for the first time. There was a large album with photographs on a varnished wood display stand. I opened it and turned the pages. I saw photographs of the concentration camps for Jews at Bergen-Belsen. I remember closing the book quickly and thinking to myself: "Now I understand everything! I understand grandpa's secret. The others were the Jews!" I ran out of the library. Shocked by my discovery, I didn't tell anyone about it but since that day, I have always sought to understand what happened, what the tragedy was that my grandfather had been forced to witness.

II

A PATH

All the major decisions in my life were made spontaneously: Faith came to me with brutal suddenness when I was 20 years old.

It was in 1976 and I was studying mathematics at Dijon University where I had met Denise, a fellow student who was never free on Thursday evenings. One day she told me that she was a Catholic and that she attended meetings in the university Catholic center. I couldn't believe it! A Catholic in a world of science . . . How, in 1976, could there still be people so old-fashioned as to believe that God could give meaning to life? I spent entire evenings explaining to her that God was merely something man had invented to reconcile himself with death. Most of my friends were Marxists or Maoists. In return, Denise and her friends spent months explaining to me why they believed in God.

A few months later, in July 1976, I was on vacation at the beach in Narbonne. Sun, sea, boredom. The loudspeakers announced the projection of a film by a Protestant group. To keep my summer apathy at bay, I went and sat in the back row. At the end of the film, two girls from the evangelical group came to talk to me about their convictions. A minute later my ship was foundering. As they spoke, for the first time in my life, I felt that Christ lived in them. I went home troubled and alone, thinking: "If Christ is alive, then it's all true, God exists!" For years I was to meditate this question: "God, what do you want?"

From then on, I sought God everywhere . . . even as far away as Calcutta. One day I found a book by Mother Teresa, *God is Love,* in which she described her life and her commitment to providing homes for the dying in Calcutta. I wrote to ask if I could help their congregation that summer. I received an airmail letter containing four words: "Come whenever you want." That response was all I needed.

The following summer I went to Bengal. Every day, I went with Mother Teresa's brothers to the home for the dying set up in Kalighat, in an annex to the temple dedicated to the goddess Kali. Men and women who lived on the street came there to die with dignity. Every day there was prayer, mass, love for the poor and for the most rejected. I saw the sisters dressed in blue and white saris kneeling on the floor of the chapel praying for food. Neighbors often arrived with bags of rice. Mother Teresa believed in this, relying on divine providence.

One day when I was ill, Mother Teresa asked to see me and, smiling warmly, she said: "Go home, recover your health and never forget, if God calls you, He will never let you go." Since then, that certainty has never left me.

I returned to France to continue my studies in mathematics. One evening, as I was climbing the stairs to my apartment, I was suddenly filled with the internal conviction that God was calling me for something specific. I began to meet with priests, with people involved in the Church. For a long time I wondered whether it was madness or if it really was a call from God.

In my search for God, I found myself in Upper Volta (now Burkina Faso) as a math teacher. I landed in Dedougou High School, which had had no math teacher for the previous two years. Every evening I went with one of the Sisters of Saint Joseph to the isolated white buildings at one end of the town. It was the leper house. Inside, in semi-obscurity, men, women, and children afflicted by the illness were waiting for us.

Thirty years later, I can still remember their smiles, but also their fear of having to return to the village. I also remember the African grandmother, Berthe, who told me that Christ had called her to look after the poorest. Berthe always said: "Patrick, when we meet the poor, we meet God." It was in Africa that I decided to become a priest.

Back in France, I entered the Prado seminary in Lyon. Everything was corroborated in the seminary. I found God in France, the same way I had found Him in India and Africa.

I became a parish priest. First I officiated in a small industrial town built by the Schneider family, Le Creusot, in Saône-et-Loire, a region not far from my family home, and then I was appointed to a parish in Lyon.

III

FROM AUSCHWITZ TO JERUSALEM

It was December 1990, I had just turned 35. The Soviet bloc was barely showing a crack. Shortly after Christmas, I went to Poland to prepare for a gathering of young people convened by Pope John Paul II in Chestokowa, a major place of pilgrimage to the Virgin Mary. When we crossed the German-Polish border, we received a wad of Polish banknotes, zlotys, in return for 500 francs. In the winter rain I saw the landscapes of the east for the first time. Little or no public lighting, empty shop windows, gray, almost identical cities, tall chimneys seen from afar, and pervasive pollution. We were driving through a country where everything seemed to be for sale, restaurants, bakeries, even the paintings in the museums. The whole country seemed to be for sale. The fissures in the Soviet system were beginning to appear. The privatizations that some hoped for were feared by others. Nobody looked at anybody else in the streets; everybody seemed to slink away, hugging the walls.

We were hosted by the family of the Polish priest who accompanied us on the trip. On the morning of December 31, 1990, several days after Lech Walesa, the leader of *Solidarnosc,* had come to power, we went to visit the main market. The stands seemed very empty to my western eyes. One stall was attracting a crowd: It boasted two exorbitantly-priced kiwis that no one could afford. The first fruit of the recently rediscovered freedom.

That evening our hosts took us to the traditional end-of-the-year mass. We set out on foot, feeling our way through the Polish night. It was cold and there was no public lighting to guide our steps. In the distance, I caught sight of the parish church, illuminated like a lighthouse in the middle of the small town. An immense queue had formed outside the entrance to the church. My Polish friends explained that there was "a mass every hour. People wait outside for the next mass because there's no room left inside." I was very impressed by the fervor and the size of the attendance at the Polish church. I had never seen such crowds in France. When I entered the sacristy, I saw three young priests dressed in golden chasubles and kneeling, deep in contemplation. They were waiting for us to celebrate the mass. I didn't understand a single word of the sermon, but I recognized one name that the priest repeated over and over again: *Solidarnosc.* On this special night, Catholic Poland was giving thanks for the years of struggle and the battle for freedom.

It was midnight when we emerged from the church. Icy rain was falling in fine droplets that solidified as soon as they hit the ground. Little by little the landscape took on a new shape, covered with a delicate layer of ice and frost. The ground was like an immense ice-skating rink. I held on to the fence on the side of the street. I slipped and recovered my balance. Used to the snow, my companions in their black plastic boots quickly left me behind. I was alone in the dark. I could barely distinguish their silhouettes so, to slow them down a little, I cried out: "Where are we now?" Someone turned round and said: "We're not far from Ukraine." I suddenly felt myself go faint in the black and icy night. I was so close to where my grandfather had been: Ukraine, Rawa-Ruska . . . The ground slipped from under my feet and I said to myself: "You've been looking for this for 50 years. You've finally found it." How could I say that when I was only 35 years old? Then I understood in a flash that I had completed a circle. That night I was cold, as my grandfather had been cold 50 years before me.

I was suddenly brutally conscious of the unfathomable nature of what it was my grandfather had tried to make me grasp: his deportation, and the Holocaust. The mists cleared from my mind. I was the grandson of Claudius Desbois, deported to camp 325. I saw the Holocaust as a responsibility: That day I understood how much the Holocaust was part of my life. The unspeakable crime to which my grandfather had been a helpless witness — the murder of men, women, and children simply because they were Jews.

Back at the house I was welcomed by the warmth of the fire and of the family that was hosting us. To celebrate the New Year we shared a few mandarin oranges and a precious box of chocolates wrapped in shiny paper. While everyone was asleep, I couldn't stop going over the obvious fact that had just struck me. I had come to prepare for a pilgrimage, and here I was, touched by a complete mystery that was a key to my own life. During that night the irrevocable decision to search took root in me. I had to understand.

After my stay in Poland, my first reaction was to learn Hebrew and to set out in search of the Jewish people. After a few months of class, my

Hebrew teacher suggested I attend a summer course at the University of Jerusalem on Mount Scopus. For two months, 210 of us went from Hebrew lessons to lectures on Jewish history and political history, singing classes, and conferences in the evening. Only two of us had return tickets for six days after the end of the course. The other student was named Charles Ben Adiba. We decided to set out together on camels for four days in the Sinai desert. I learned more during that stay than in all my lessons on Judaism. Charles was observant and said the psalms three times each day. I knew nothing about Jewish traditions. He explained why he put on the *talith,*[1] and why he wound the *tefillin*[2] around his arm. He explained the reasons and rules governing kosher food.

Upon our return from Israel I met his family and became friends with them. Whenever I go to Paris, I stay with them in Créteil. The Ben Adiba are a traditional Sepharadic family originally from Algiers. Charles sometimes took me with him and his friends to attend the courses, always densely packed, given by Grand Rabbi Gilles Bernheim.[3] Day after day, I learned about living Judaism.

The following year I enrolled in the French-language seminars at Yad Vashem.[4] There, I spent 10 days learning the history of anti-Semitism. For me, having always lived in a family environment that was immune to all forms of anti-Semitism, the first sessions were profoundly shocking. I learned about pogroms, expulsions, ghettoes, yellow stars, and the Holocaust. I learned that before Auschwitz there had been Operation Reinhardt[5] and the *Einsatzgruppen.*[6]

I had such an urge to understand that I attended this seminar for seven years in a row.

In October 1992, I was appointed Superior of the Prado Seminary in Lyon. I looked for activities that would make me feel at home in the city. I naturally turned to the archbishop of Lyon, Cardinal Decourtray, whom I had met in Dijon where he had been bishop when I was rediscovering the Catholic faith. At the time, he had celebrated mass in a rather peculiar way: cancer had made him mute and others preached and read his texts. It was very impressive. Some time later he recovered his speech and became archbishop of Lyon.

When he received me at 1, Place de Fourvière, on the hill overlooking the city, the interview lasted only 20 minutes. I asked for his advice on my activities. He replied without hesitation: "The Jewish community. Charles Favre, my advisor on the Touvier[7] affair, was recently kidnapped and then released . . . He is marked by his experience, but he is recovering his strength. He will train you. Ask my secretary to call him." In a few minutes I found myself in his secretary's office as she called Charles Favre. Dr. Favre's reputation was well-known: he was said to be detestable, an ogre who devoured whomever came in front of him. I asked for an appointment, which he granted only months later. He finally received me on the first floor of a bourgeois building on the Boulevard Maréchal-de-Saxe. I rang at a reinforced door with a multitude of names on it. The apartment had two entrances so that the doctor could see who was ringing the bell. He opened the door very slowly and I found myself facing a small man with round, lively eyes. He preceded me through an immense apartment, furnished only with bookshelves rising from floor to ceiling, and filled with perfectly classified files, books, and reviews. No other furniture. The only decoration, beyond rather old radios with chronometers, included five or six television sets, each with a VCR. He explained that each set was tuned to a different station: "I study public opinion. I record programs and I fill in grids on public opinion." After passing through this strange universe, I finally sat down facing him, as he installed himself behind his desk, piled high with books and newspapers. His telephone never stopped ringing. He began a long monologue. We sat for hours without moving. He told me everything, from his discovery of God thanks to the Jews, to his decision to serve the Catholic Church, his training in the United States in political and economic forecasting, his service under Cardinal Villot during Vatican Council II, his role with the cardinal in getting the Jewish refuseniks out of the Soviet Union, his role with Cardinal Decourtray in the case of the Auschwitz Convent, the Touvier case, the Barbie case, his meetings with Paul VI, John-Paul I, and John-Paul II, his meeting with his leader Jean Monnet, and so on. After seven hours, I finally dared to interrupt him to tell him I'd be back the next day.

My legs still stiff, I found myself on the pavement of the Boulevard Maréchal-de-Saxe wondering what I had gotten myself into. A whole new universe was opening up for me.

Four or five times a week I went to see Dr. Favre, who had agreed to train me. We saw each other for one or two hours each day, and often met his friends for lunch, Dr. Marc Aron, and Alain Jakubowicz.[8] We discussed world affairs, and Dr. Favre gave me an understanding of public opinion, geopolitics, geo-strategy, and also of the Jewish people. He taught me to see them as the people of the Covenant, and how to position myself as a Catholic in an ethical context that was faithful to John-Paul II and to Vatican Council II, while respecting the Jewish religion and people. He shared with me his prayers, his eucharistic devotion, and his faith in the saints.

After training me for two years, he began to introduce me to the Jewish community. He taught me everything I needed to know about the traditions, the practices, and the history of the Jewish people.

Through him I also discovered the Brooklyn Jews of America, and the Diaspora.

In the meantime, thanks to this training, I had become one of Cardinal Decourtray's leading mediators in his relations with Jewish representatives. I met many Jews: laymen, believers, practicing Jews, and ultra-orthodox Jews. I always bear Cardinal Decourtray's words in mind: "You must never discriminate between the Jews; we did too much of that during the war."

Alongside these teachings I also assiduously studied the words and actions of Pope John-Paul II in relation to Judaism and the Jews. In the last 60 years since World War II we have overcome centuries of incomprehension, although the understanding between the Jews and the Catholic Church is still a rather fragile construct.

Charles Favre also inspired me with his praying, so simple it is almost child-like. He used to tell me: stand before God every day, sometimes obstinately. He likes to repeat: when a situation becomes too difficult, it is imperative to pray, pray, and pray again. When he has a major problem, he telephones the Carmelite Sisters of Jerusalem installed on Mount Olivet, and asks them to pray for him. I have adopted this same habit. Without prayer, theirs and mine, I never could have persevered in my mission.

IV

THE PRIEST OF BELZEC

After attending several seminars at Yad Vashem, I decided that I had to visit the actual sites of the Shoah. I took on the organization of a travel group with the following program: three days in Auschwitz, three days studying Operation Reinhardt, and one day in Ukraine to study the *Einsatzgruppen*. At each stage we called on experts. Numerous friends accompanied me on the trip: Richard Prasquier, president of Yad Vashem France; Jean-François Bodin, head of communications of the francophone Radios Chrétiennes; Levana Franck, an Israeli historian, and many others.

In Auschwitz, one of the experts I worked with was Marcello Pezzetti.[1] Once we were both in Jerusalem, we were walking on Ben Yehuda street in Jerusalem one evening, when Marcello stopped and said: "You see, Patrick, I don't study the Auschwitz camp; I live in the camp." Every year he drives there in his Fiat with his wife and daughter.

At the site in Auschwitz, Marcello used archival photos to explain that at Auschwitz, the Jews had disembarked from the trains at the

Judenrampe,[2] the place of selection. Those who were selected for death were taken to bunkers I and II, two former farms that had been transformed into gas chambers by the Nazis.

Today, on that spot there are three buildings side by side. During one Christmas there, the Goldstein family, who are Swiss Jews, told me how a Polish family had built their house on the foundations of bunker I. We were facing the houses, in the snow, when Mr. Goldstein told me, "You know, Patrick, this is proof that ghosts don't exist." Three families live an ordinary life there, with laundry drying in the windows, smoke coming out of the chimneys, children playing on swings, and chickens running around. There is nothing to indicate that 110,000 people died there.

Our journey continued to Belzec, a village close to the Ukrainian border. A camp was established there, and more than 500,000 Jews were taken there in cattle cars. All that remains of the camp is an overgrown field in the middle of the village, with bones sticking out of the ground—the only evidence of the extermination machine that was created here.

Once in the hotel-restaurant, I was advised to go and talk to the village priest who was aged 91 and would have seen everything. I went to meet him, accompanied by my interpreter and Richard Prasquier. The priest told us how, during the war, he would go up on the roof with binoculars and watch, along with the other inhabitants of the village, the executions in the camp. I asked him: "Did it not affect you, Father, to watch all those people die?" He replied: "Yes. My mother couldn't bear the smoke. So when there was too much smoke, she shut herself up in the cellar and I had to look after her." Richard Prasquier became visibly agitated, but I continued as if nothing were amiss. I wanted to know. I would have never imagined that people had watched these executions willingly. There were paintings hanging on the walls in a corridor of the priest's house. As I got up to them, I realized they were miniature reproductions of the camp. One of them depicted naked Jews waiting in front of the doors of the gas chamber; one could even make out beds of red flowers planted in front of the entrance. In another, an excavator carried the bodies to be burnt. I turned and asked the priest: "Who made these?" In an even tone, he replied: "A madman . . ."

Once outside, we returned to the restaurant, where a bowl of hot soup, containing very fatty meat, awaited us. The waitress told us that during the war they couldn't clean the windows; they were so greasy with the smoke. I vomited during much of that night. I realized that everyone had seen the executions. In my family, the Shoah was a secret, but not in Belzec. I had thought that nobody could see inside the extermination camps, that they were like secret bases . . . Now, I realized that they were a part of everyday life. I learned that passenger trains never stopped running during the war, during the extermination and cremation of the Jews. Passengers were simply advised to close their windows before passing the camp, to block out the smell.

In Belzec I met the baker who delivered the bread for the camp staff, the carpenter who made the gas chamber, and the daughter of the mayor of Belzec. Her father had been chosen by the head of the extermination camp to lead a temporary town hall. Every day, he had to meet the head of the camp and discuss provisions: the camp needed barbed wire, staff, and horses. The SS stables had been bombed, so the head of the camp asked the mayor to bring 40 horses to the main square. A German veterinarian inspected them and chose the best 18; each farmer who owned a requisitioned horse was given a ticket to allow him to get it back eventually. I met the son of one of these farmers. As the war dragged on, his father got worried and went to the camp with his ticket to collect his horse. He talked about how his father had seen the ash mills operating in the camp, old agricultural machines that were used to sort wheat from other grains. The Nazis used them to ventilate the ashes from the bodies, and to find dental gold.

I realized then that there are witnesses to the Shoah who are not Jewish: neither perpetrators nor victims, but witnesses. Was Pope John Paul II himself not one of the witnesses to the disappearance of the Jewish community in Wadowice, his hometown? He gave this testimony during his visit to Yad Vashem in Jerusalem on March 23, 2000.

The following day, we crossed the Polish-Ukrainian border. After a seemingly interminable wait of six hours in the torrential rain, we were authorized to enter Ukraine and we arrived at Rawa-Ruska. Finally, the place I had wondered about for so many years had become a reality. We saw the low houses with red roofs. I wanted to find the memorial of camp 325, where my grandfather had been interned. I was taken to a hill from where I could see a very dirty vertical white stone: the stone memorial for my grandfather's camp. Despite the steepness of the slope and the mud, I descended, alone. Nothing remains of the camp, just the stone. I took several photographs of this poor monument as a migraine overwhelmed me.

———————

Back in France, I started looking for survivors of the Rawa-Ruska camp. I found the address of the association for camp survivors. They give me a very warm welcome, and when they saw my pictures of the memorial, their reaction was immediate: "A new memorial must be created." One suggested we meet again. His name was René Chevalier, nephew of Maurice Chevalier, the famous French singer. We decided to return to Rawa-Ruska, together with his wife, daughter, and a friend.

V

FROM CEMETERY TO CEMETERY

In June 2002, I left for Rawa-Ruska with René Chevalier and his family. We landed in Lviv, a large Austro-Hungarian city. The airport is basic. This is where René had worked during his detention, filling the holes in the runways. As we walked down from the plane René said to me: "We always worked next to a group of Jews who came on foot from the Lviv ghetto. Every night fewer Jews returned to the ghetto than had come in the morning." When I asked him where the dead were buried, René answered: "You know, there were many holes in the airport runway at that time . . ."

We went straight to Rawa-Ruska. René Chevalier wanted to walk the route he had taken all those years ago after his hurried descent from the train to the camp. He found the place where he was thrown from the train, and the little path that he had taken to cross the village. I was moved and surprised by his ability to find his way, more than 50 years later. "Here was the ghetto. The Jews seemed so sad," he murmured, as he walked, taking long strides. I didn't know then that Rawa-Ruska (the name means "Rawa the Russian"), was nicknamed "Rawa the Jewish" before the war, so numerous were its Jewish inhabitants. Ukrainian grandmothers, understanding what we were looking for, pointed out the way. Not much seemed to have changed in this sleepy little town. When we got to the town, the municipal authorities showed us the site of the monument to the French camp. Noticing René's astonishment at not being able to see the camp, they explained that "there are no more buildings. The camp doesn't exist any more." When we asked them why, the municipal authorities balked, insisting that nothing remained of the Rawa-Ruska internment camp. René insisted: "That's not possible! The buildings were very large." We decided to go and look for the site ourselves, and discovered, to our amazement, that the camp had never been destroyed.

The camp of Rawa-Ruska[1] covered 45 hectares, and was composed of a multitude of *unterlager* (sub-camps) to which the deported were assigned. The first prisoners arrived on April 13, 1942. After the war, the camp was used for German prisoners, and eventually as barracks, first for the Soviet and then the Ukrainian military. How could such a large expanse be hidden from the view of former deportees returning to the place of their internment? Very simply by detouring them to the memorial, about 300 meters away from the site. This is, to me, one of the great mysteries in Eastern Europe: it has been my repeated experience that things pertaining to the war are officially invisible. Even though the traces truly exist and are blatantly visible to anyone who would look, an illusion is created: as if, arriving at the gates of Auschwitz, one met people claiming that there were no traces of the camp left, and everyone believed them.

Throughout my research for this project, I was often told that the camps, the ghettoes, the synagogues, and the stones of the Jewish cemeteries had disappeared, and that nothing remained. Eventually, I no longer paid any attention to these claims, and looked, with dogged determination, for the ghettoes, the synagogues, and the stones of the Jewish cemeteries by myself. I always found them.

At the end of our visit, we were received by the mayor in a tiny office on the second floor of a grey building. From a metal cupboard, he brought out two little flags, one French, and the other Ukrainian, along with a bottle of red Georgian wine, and gave us a speech worthy of the great occasions of the Soviet era, ending, inevitably, with: "Long live France! Long live Ukraine! Long live the French-Ukrainian friendship!"

At the end of this theatrical celebration, I approached his desk and asked him: "Mr. Mayor, where were all the Jews from the village buried?" The mayor turned to stare at me and then, with an absent air, said: "We don't know anything about that." He got up and went back to exclaiming: "Long live France! Long live Ukraine! Long live the French-Ukrainian friendship!" I realized I would learn nothing from him. Everyone seemed to be ignorant of—or eager to hide—the very existence of the 10,000 Jews who had been shot in this little town back in 1942. Ten thousand people shot cannot go unnoticed. I come from a small village and I know that if one person had been shot there, everyone would remember it—imagine 10,000!

Returning to the memorial with René Chevalier, we discovered the large mass graves into which the bodies of the Soviet prisoners of camp 325 were thrown. From July 1941 to April 1942, about 18,000 prisoners were locked up there. All died in atrocious conditions. It is said that at Rawa-Ruska many were bludgeoned to death with clubs. A witness recounts how "every day, Russian bulldozers would emerge carrying the bodies of Soviet prisoners. They were taken to the forest where immense pits awaited them. Two Soviet prisoners were forced to arrange the bodies in the pit."[2] The Soviets were buried in the forest just behind the camp, 100 meters above it. We could barely make out the traces of the pits, hidden under a meter of brambles. René Chevalier was visibly moved; he explained: "When we arrived, the Soviet prisoners had just been killed and the camp was empty. The Germans forced the Jews of the ghetto to remove their corpses." He told me that when they entered the camp, they were forbidden to go into the buildings, which were sealed with planks of wood. They lost no time in removing the bodies and, when they did so, found the walls of the rooms covered with bits of brain and blood: it was there that the Nazis had killed the last Soviet prisoners.

When I asked René Chevalier if he had seen Jews being assassinated, his eyes clouded over. With a voice full of restrained emotion, he started to talk, with a fixed gaze that looked far into the distance. He had witnessed the requisition of Jewish women to do the harvesting as there were no more animals to pull the carts filled with hay. They came in the morning with their children. The German who was guarding them could not stand their crying and whenever it irritated him too much, he would get hold of a little child and bludgeon it to death against a cart. In the evening, all that remained were the women, carts, and hay.

The French prisoners were condemned to witness the genocide of the Jews. They were condemned to see their murders.

I went back to Rawa-Ruska the following year, in June 2003, for the inauguration of the new memorial of camp 325 that we had organized. By then I had made up my mind to find the mass graves of the Jews. At the end of the ceremony, I asked if there were still Jews in Rawa-Ruska. A very well-dressed woman with a straw hat came up to me shyly and said: "I am the Jewish community of Rawa-Ruska. I am a retired teacher and the last Jew of Rawa-Ruska." It was as though Chokhina had always been waiting for us. She couldn't tell me about the graves, though, because she was born after the war.

After the ceremony, the new mayor of Rawa-Ruska received us in his restaurant, the Hermes. His wife, an interior decorator, had just repainted the establishment from floor to ceiling, and all the walls were covered in characters from Greek mythology, hardly a typical sight in this ruined and severely under-developed town. We were offered a sumptuous meal with caviar, smoked meats, and Georgian wines. At the other end of the room, a family in traditional Ukrainian dress provided music. The mother and her children, two sets of female and male twins, formed a choir. One of the male twins, Maxim, played the accordion in a very particular style, and I thought I could make out Jewish melodies. When the accordionist approached our table, I asked him if he knew what had happened to the Jews of the village. He replied: "Since I was a child, I've been fascinated with the Jewish past of the villages in the region. I found an old book that told their story. I spent my whole youth looking for where the Jews lived. If you want, I can show you." I was stunned. Maxim put down his accordion and invited us to join him outside. At the wheel of an old burgundy-colored car, he took us across the badly asphalted little country roads.

We went to Ougnif, an old village where many Jews lived. The synagogue was still there, or at least its walls were: An enormous red brick building with, next door, what was the *cheder* (the Torah school). The *cheder* had now been converted into a technical school, whereas the synagogue was used as a storehouse for agricultural machinery and wheat. I was stupefied. I turned to Maxim and asked: "Do you know many more places like this?"

"Of course," he replied, "there is a Jewish cemetery a little further on."

We went back into the car, and continued on the bumpy road until we arrived at a depot locked behind iron gates and filled with large red agricultural machines typical of the Soviet Union. Nothing that resembled a cemetery! Sensing our skepticism, Maxim indicated the entrance with insistence. The cemetery had become invisible to everyone's eyes, but not to his.

My thoughts suddenly drifted toward Lublin in Poland, where I had met someone like Maxim. Before the war, Lublin was composed of two areas, like two lungs: a Christian area and a Jewish area. The Nazis had established the headquarters of Operation Reinhardt there. There was no selection in those camps. Day and night, the cattle trucks arrived, Jews got out and were gassed. In the Christian area, the Reich had set up a veritable SS city. The Jewish quarter of Lublin was entirely destroyed, and today the town looks like a bird who has had one wing amputated. There I had met a young Pole, born well after the war, who had created a little Jewish museum in the spot where the two districts converged. The black and white photos inside were the only proof of the existence of a Jewish quarter before the war. Every house in the ghetto had been photographed, and he had organized the images by following the house numbers in the street. A little further on, in a small room, a large model made out of colored cardboard had pride of place. He had reconstructed all the houses of the town.

In Lublin, as in Ougnif, the grandsons of Ukrainians and of Poles were bringing back to life the memory of their Jewish neighbors who had disappeared under the Nazi regime.

Maxim interrupted the thread of my memories. "There is also the cemetery of the Germans," he said. Taken aback, I asked him to take us there. The cemetery was about 15 kilometers away. The road was asphalted and well maintained, and the surroundings lush. Maxim told us: "This road is very particular. Everyone here says that it brings bad luck. It was made by the Soviets with the sand from the Jewish cemetery of Rawa-Ruska. You know, there are a lot of accidents on this road, and people say that the road should not have been built with the bones of the dead."

We parked in front of the entrance to the German cemetery, in the district of Potelych. The cemetery is huge—a pretty landscape stretched out over hundreds of meters. It is spread out over several hillocks, on each of which three thick crosses of cut stone have been erected. A warden, who was a little drunk, appeared and explained: "The bodies of all the Germans who were killed in Ukraine during the Second World War are being reburied here. There," he said, pointing to a long open ditch, "I am waiting for 4,407 bodies of Germans from Ternopil. Their names are known from the metallic medallion they wore, which have been sent to Berlin. And they are going to make a wall of names by company: the Wehrmacht, the Waffen-SS, or the SS. The bodies are first held in Zhouvkva until enough of them are collected. Each body is buried in an individual cardboard coffin." The warden then showed us a list of all the bodies that had already come to him. On each line was the medallion number and a brief description of the human remains found. I asked him who was behind this initiative. "It's a private German foundation that wants all the Germans to be decently buried. We are launching an appeal in every region. For example, if a family buried a German in the garden after a battle, they get in touch with us, and we go to look for it. I will show you the bottom of the cemetery: it is the SS square."

He led us to an enormous granite cross with two crosses on either side towers over the far end of the cemetery. Stuffed toys seem to have been recently laid on one of these monuments. One inscription reads: "To our grandfather, who was so kind."

While the mass graves of the thousands of Jews who were shot are untraceable, every German killed during the war has been reburied and identified by name. The cemeteries are on the scale of the Reich. Magnificent cemeteries for the Germans, including the SS, little graves for the French, white stones covered in brambles for the tens of thousands of anonymous Soviet soldiers, and absolutely nothing for the Jews.

Thus, under the ground, everything is still in order according to the hierarchy of the Reich. We cannot give a posthumous victory to Nazism. We cannot leave the Jews buried like animals. We cannot accept this state of affairs and allow our continent to be built on the obliterated memory of the victims of the Reich.

Maxim continued acting as our guide. He showed us the old Jewish cemetery of Rawa-Ruska which had been turned into a large sandpit. The sand was brought there in 1952 during the Soviet period. All that remains of the cemetery is a wall. All the Jewish stones that could be found were placed out of the way on top of each other, to form a pile that was hard to reach, between a pit filled with water and the trees. That is all that remains of the Jews of Rawa-Ruska.

The following morning, we went back to the Hermes restaurant, where the deputy mayor of Rawa-Ruska, Yaroslav, tapped me on the shoulder: "Patrick, we are waiting for you." We went out and got into his black, air-conditioned car. We left the village, the houses became more and more spread apart. We went down a muddy track, then passed a pond surrounded by green huts. I had no idea where we were going. Yaroslav had not said a word since we had left the restaurant.

Five kilometers further on we came to a small sign that read "Borove." We were in a hamlet, or rather a widening in the hardened dirt road with, on either side, a row of traditional houses painted in white and blue. The silence was disturbed only by the barking of little dogs, and the clacking of a flock of white geese. Not a soul was in sight.

As we were coming out of Borove, I saw a group of a hundred or so elderly people at a bend of the road. They seemed to be waiting for us, standing there stoically, propped up by sticks. In the car, Yaroslav broke the silence: "We are going to the mass grave of the last Jews of Rawa-Ruska." My emotions were at a breaking point. I wondered who the old people might be, looking so miserable, and wearing dark green oilskins and plastic boots filled with newspaper, some accompanied by their goat tied to the end of a rope.

As soon as we got out of the car, in silence, the group started making its way toward the end of the village. I followed them. We walked together, leaving the village, turning off to the right, and entering a forest by a path that had been newly cleared. Recently cut brambles lay strewn across the ground. The deputy mayor explained that a friend who is a forest-worker had tidied the trail so that we could walk across the forest. We came to a clearing, at the bottom of which we saw an earth mound about a meter high, 10 meters long, and five meters wide, covered in greenery. Yaroslav said to me: "Here is the mass grave of the last Jews killed in Rawa-Ruska." My eyes misted over and I lowered my head. I thought of my grandfather and his silences. I thought above all of those who were brought here, behind this hamlet, and assassinated 60 years ago. I had finally found those "others" of whom my grandfather had spoken. "For the others, it was worse . . ."

Svetlana, my interpreter, was holding a little book entitled *The Holocaust at Rawa-Ruska*,[3] written in Russian in 1944, which the mayor had given her. It laid out the conclusions of the Soviet commission regarding what had happened at Borove. Svetlana began reading aloud to these country people the official version of what happened. "In April 1943, the camp of the town of Mosty Wielkie, in which there were more than 1,200 Jewish people, was transferred to the town of Rawa-Ruska. In the night of November 10, 1943, the fascist oppressors surrounded the camp and transported all the people to Borove, in rural Soviet Union, where they were shot and the bodies buried in a large pit."[4] As I listened to Svetlana, I realized that it was here that the 1,200 last Jews of the *Judenlager*[5] of Rawa-Ruska were executed.

In a rather authoritarian manner, the deputy mayor arranged the witnesses in a semi-circle in front of the pit. Each one had brought an animal—a goat, a goose, or a dog. One by one, like children in a class, they went into the middle of the circle to tell their story of what they had seen in this place in 1941.

The first went forward and said: "I saw the execution of the last Jews, shot by the Germans. They brought them here in trucks. I remember the blood that ran like a stream after the execution, along the path that goes down to the village. The Germans asked me to come and cover the pit with chalk to dry the ground out; it smelt so bad." A small, frail woman stepped forward and started speaking; she was crying: "The Germans had grenades that they threw in the pit after the shooting of the Jews because many of them were not dead yet. One day I saw the dismembered body of a woman on the top of a tree. That tree you can see over there. They made me climb up in the tree to bring the body down and put it in the pit." She fell silent and withdrew, in tears, her face buried in her hands.

Others spoke, each in turn. Every one of them recalled things more horrible than the last. And I stood there, stunned, unable to move, listening to these people delivering the secret of the Shoah in this village. I had only one desire: to scream and beg them to stop. But no one could stop what was happening. Each one of them was narrating, for the first time, the history of the execution of the last Jews of Rawa-Ruska, the assassination of young people whose children and parents had already been killed. I realized that the memory of the genocide existed, and that it was humble people, country farmers, who carried it. The Jewish woman we had met was also present, clearly overwhelmed with emotion. The following day she was waiting for us, standing, outside her house, her feet in the mud, with a bouquet of white lilies, and a book by Saint-Exupéry in Russian that she wanted to give me. "I am giving you this book because I am going to move. My husband has just died and I am going to join my children." The last Jew of Rawa-Ruska was leaving.

At the end of that day, while the deputy mayor was accompanying me back to town, he suddenly spoke up, issuing what was both a challenge and promise: "Patrick, this is what I could do for one village; I can do the same thing for a hundred villages." Without hesitating or reflecting, I replied: "Alright! Let's do it!"

Gregory Havan, 76, Borove, Lviv region, April 25, 2004

Patrick Debois: Do you remember when the Germans arrived in Rawa-Ruska?

G.H.: Yes. The first time they came was in September 1939. Then again in 1941.

P.D.: What happened?

G.H.: The war had been going on for two weeks in Poland. The war hadn't arrived here yet, just several planes that bombed the station of Rawa-Ruska. Then the German troops came, the soldiers on motorbikes. With the other children, we went to see the soldiers, barefoot, like beggars. The Jews were frightened. They didn't go to see them but went to hide. The soldiers didn't shoot but gave the children sweets—though instead of giving them to us in our hands, they threw them on the ground. They stayed two weeks. After that, they knew they would have to give up territory. They bought us things; we were poor at the time. A soldier told us that they wouldn't stay long, that they would leave again for the west and that the Russians would soon arrive.

P.D.: How did they create the ghetto?

G.H.: On June 22, 1941, the war began and planes started bombing us. The border was only 15 kilometers away. Shooting began. Wounded Russians were brought in on wooden stretchers. Then the Germans arrived. We didn't have a *kolkhoze* here, so the Germans came and asked all the farm owners to give a bag of 100 kilos of potatoes. I remember I helped my father put the potatoes in a bag. They were for the Jews in the ghetto of Rawa-Ruska. It was all they would have to eat during the whole winter.

They had ordered all the Jews in the village to wear an armband on their right arm with the star of David. The cloth was white and the star black. The Jews had to give up the milk from their cows and also their cows. Then they were taken to Rawa. There, they were shot; there was a cremation oven. The Jews were frightened. The Jews of our village, including one of my colleagues, were all taken.

P.D.: What were they made to do?

G.H.: I'll tell you what I remember. In Rawa, the Jews lived all over town, in every street. There wasn't a Jewish neighborhood. Then it was decreed they should all live together and that they shouldn't live with Catholics. They were all told to gather in the middle of town, all crowded in together.

P.D.: What happened to the empty houses?

G.H.: They made a ghetto on a single street, where no one was allowed to enter. We weren't allowed to bring things in but we did it anyway. Jews gave us money for a chicken or something else. They began by shooting old people and children. They left people between the ages of 18 and 45 to make them work. Three kilometers away, they killed them; people fell like flies. I didn't see them but I heard the shots. I saw a young Jew who brought corpses in a cart to the Jewish cemetery. It was during the winter of 1942. There was blood and the ground was red.

P.D.: Why did they choose Borove as the location to shoot the Jews?

G.H.: I don't know. In June 1943, a German officer came with a dog, to visit the village then left after a quarter of an hour. The following morning, very early, perhaps at 6 or 7 o'clock, the Jewish police arrived with a tractor and a truck. Then, perhaps one or two hours later, trucks full of people arrived. People were sitting in the trucks. They were accompanied by Ukrainian and Jewish police. They had brought the people to this place. The people were sitting in the truck and the police were guarding them with rifles. I remember that a girl tried to escape by jumping from the truck; she was shot in the forest.

P.D.: How were the Jews shot?

G.H.: I don't know, we weren't allowed to go there. I know that the trucks arrived one after the other. Afterwards there were shots.

P.D.: But afterwards, did they requisition people to bury them?

G.H.: The Jews dug the pits themselves. We went there the next day and the pits were covered with a thin layer of earth. I don't know if the Germans did that themselves. Very soon afterwards, blood began running from the pit. Toward 5 or 6 in the evening, we began to smell an odor and then, as it smelled of death, they forced people who had carts and horses to bring sand there. They also put chlorine. That allowed them to lower the level of the pit by one meter and the blood stopped running.

P.D.: After that, did the Germans continue guarding the place?

G.H.: No. Everyone could go there. Because the Jews had undressed there and people saw the Germans taking the civilian clothes of women and men, they came to see if they could find something: money, rings, gold watches . . . From time to time, the policemen threw them a coat. And they found things—they even found American dollars. The Jews had hidden all these things in the ground. After that, people didn't go there anymore and a forest began to grow in the place that used to be a field.

P.D.: Did people come to say Jewish prayers there?

G.H.: When the Russians arrived, there were no more than five Jews, who left after the war. No one came to say a prayer. People came to see the pit and they walked around the area, but that's all.

VI

A TEAM AND ITS ETHIC

In my search for other Ukrainian witnesses, I surrounded myself with people who became, over time, my team—a team that comprised ten individual personalities, from ten different backgrounds. Ten people whose paths had crossed.

First came Svetlana Biryulova, my interpreter. A pivotal and indispensable character whom I had met on my first trip to the Ukraine. She was waiting for me at the airport with Yaroslav, a former pilot who drove a small blue Renault Estafette. From then on, we were inseparable. Svetlana was an art historian of Russian origin and knew everything about the former USSR. She often acted as a guide for foreign sports delegations when they traveled in the Soviet republics. Her husband's collection of beautiful paintings of Jewish art in Ukraine was exhibited at the Lviv art museum. When she took me to visit the museum, I was struck by the large paintings, particularly those by St. Fabianski depicting the Kiev pogrom of 1905.[1] A multitude of small paintings portrayed the diversity and richness of Jewish culture through its artists, lay people, and the devout . . . 2,700,000 people who disappeared between 1941 and 1944.

Svetlana understood, like no one else, how to gently approach an elderly person seated on a bench or walking along the road. She knew how to go into a witness's house with discretion and warmth, how to walk a while with an old Ukrainian woman going to the market before we could come on with our questions. Svetlana was the advance guard, who within half an hour of meeting a witness might be cooking with her in the kitchen or at least carrying her shopping bags. She prepared the ground, taking the time necessary to win trust. No one could be afraid of Svetlana.

One morning I asked her what was the first question she asked a witness. She replied, in her charming Russian accent: "I always ask: 'Did you live here during the war?' If the person answers 'Yes,' I say to them, 'Then you will be able to help us!'" It seems simple, but it requires a great skill that blended audacity and respect. If you didn't know her, you would think that Svetlana was a member of each of all the Ukrainian villages that we were passing through. Within a few minutes, she was able to become part of the landscape.

Svetlana was also the one who was most moved and terrified when we approached the pits and found the bones of the assassinated Jews, scattered through the grass by grave robbers.

_____

Mikhailo "Micha" Strutinsky was our ballistics expert. I met him in Lviv, in the market located in the old town, not far from the opera and the church of the protecting Virgin. The market was pompously named "Arts Market," but all that it sold was souvenirs, such as table-cloths and white shirts decorated with traditional embroidery. One could also find some paintings, all fairly worthless, done by former students of the Lviv art school, which were placed directly on the ground in the square, and covered with clear plastic to protect them from the rain that is so frequent in that region. There were also people selling secondhand goods on low metal folding tables, heaped high with every kind of real and imitation Soviet watch, Red Army armbands, military caps, and Polish, Russian, and Ukrainian coins. One stall specialized in *matriochkas,* the famous Russian dolls, a series of figurines carved out of fine, hand-painted wood, each fitting inside the other. The dolls usually depict Ukrainian traditional figures, but often you could find a special one, also hand-painted, with the biggest doll showing Putin's face and, inside, Yeltsin, Gorbachev, Brezhnev, Khrushchev, then Stalin, and, finally, the smallest doll in solid wood: Lenin. In this market people mainly sell small objects, the scattered remains of a society that no longer exists. Among this bric-a-brac one can find the fragments of a time that endures only in people's memory. I also found photographs of Galician villages.

One morning, one of the vendors at the market introduced me to Micha, a specialist in ballistics and anthropology. When the introductions were over, I asked him if he knew of the mass graves. He said yes. We immediately left for the place he knew. Micha is 6 feet 2 inches tall, has very short grey hair, and usually dresses in khaki army gear and combat boots. He outpaced Svetlana and me by several strides. Both Svetlana—who was wearing a red and black outfit and was not used to this kind of exercise—and I were soon out of breath as we climbed the steep hill. We clung to whatever branches we could to help us move forward. We went deeper and deeper into the forest and crossed a cleared trail, full of newly cut wood. After long minutes of walking in the wood, Micha stopped. He put his bag down on the ground and, without even looking at us, said: "It's here!" I asked him how he knew; his only response was to move his right hand to point out to the bone of a child's shoulder blade, marked with a bullet hole, lying on the earth. Further on we found a half-buried human skull, the jaws torn off. And, further still, on the left, a human femur sticking out of the ground.

Micha became the one who, day after day, with exemplary conscientiousness, located the pits, found cartridge cases, and helped us track down witnesses. Sometimes the absurd and the tragic collided. One day, while we were looking for a witness in the village of Hlibochok where there was apparently no mass grave, we saw an old man with a black cap coming toward us on a beige bicycle, pedaling very slowly. Micha went toward him and called out: "Hello, grandfather, were you there the day the Jews were executed?" He replied, without pausing his pedaling, "Of course I was there. But I don't have time now." And with that he continued on his route, and was about to cycle round us when Micha gently stopped him and made him get off his bike. Putting it under his arm, Micha called over to a neighbor who was watching us, planted in the middle of the courtyard of his farm, and said to him: "Look after the bike for a couple of hours; we're coming back." And, without a word, the grandfather climbed into our van.

He took us to a mass grave of Jews, a pit a hundred meters away from the village, in full view among cultivated fields. It was a huge circular hole into which, before the war, sick cows and sheep were thrown when they died. That was where the Germans shot all the members of the Jewish community. After the war, the village continued throwing the bodies of horses and sick animals into it. Therefore, in this hole there were the bodies of animals, then of human beings and on top more animals. Two hours later, Micha collected the bike and helped the old man onto it. He went on his way on the dirt road, as if nothing had happened.

Guillaume Ribot, our photographer, was also part of this adventure. Originally from Grenoble, he was the child of a Protestant family on one side, and a Catholic one on the other. Several members of his family had hidden Jews during the war and had been deported to Auschwitz and to Buchenwald, where some of them had had to work in the crematoriums. He had published a book of photographs on the camp at Auschwitz[2] and was preparing another on the internment camps in France.[3] He had participated in one of the itinerant courses on the Shoah that I had organized. Several days after the beginning of that trip in Wlodowa, Poland, I saw Guillaume sitting on a bench by himself, away from the group, opposite the old synagogue not far from the Belorussian border. He said: "Everything has changed for me. I didn't think I would meet Ukrainians who witnessed these events. I also didn't know that the bodies of the Jews had never been buried. I was taking pictures of camps, pieces of barbed wire while here we have living people who remember and the bodies of their Jewish neighbors who were never buried." He remained silent on the bench for a very long time. He agreed to become the photographer for our expeditions.

In each encounter with a witness of the Holocaust by bullets there was a moment, sometimes brief, where the person was no longer with us. He or she was there, 60 years earlier, hidden in a bush, or perched in an oak tree, not far from the pit where Jews awaited their death, where they were assassinated.

Thanks to his special sight and the mastery of his art, Guillaume was able to capture that moment, without voyeurism but with respect. He managed to express the emotion of the witnesses in his photographs of them. With him, I could capture the expressions of the witnesses and their eyes that had seen such horrors.

Various cameramen succeeded each other. They all used their holidays to come to Ukraine. You have to be dedicated to get up at dawn, breakfast on sliced bacon and boiled eggs, and listen to Ukrainian peasants telling of the horror until late into the evening. It was a miracle to meet friends who were willing to devote a summer or a Christmas to collecting, in small villages without water or electricity, the voices of those men and women who wanted people to remember that in their home, behind the church, all the Jews were shot one morning in the summer of 1942.

In my team there also was a young researcher, Andrej Umansky, who studied the archives. A young Ukrainian living in Germany, when I met him he was a volunteer at the museum of the children of Izieu, a project that commemorated the 44 Jewish children of the orphanage at Izieu in France who were deported and murdered.

Andrej came on the first journey with us. He was returning to this Ukraine of the Shoah, from which his parents had fled, for the first time as an adult. His last name was Uman, the name of a town in Ukraine. During this trip we passed through Bilatserkva, where his grandmother lived. His surprise was great: Bilatserkva is a town south of Kiev that has the unfortunate distinction of being the place where the Nazis decided to assassinate Jewish children, like in Izieu.[4] In this town, adult Jews had already been assassinated, and 90 children were deposited in a school, without water and food, in atrocious conditions, with no one to look after them. Numerous reports were drawn up by Protestant and Catholic clerics of the Wehrmacht protesting against this situation. This is when Paul Blobel[5] arrived with a letter from the *Gauleiter*[6] proclaiming that he had not only the authorization but also the duty to kill the children for "these children will be tomorrow's enemies."[7] The children were packed into a truck. But the German SS refused to shoot them, so the dirty task was entrusted to inexperienced Ukrainians.

Andrej said to me: "To think that when I was a child I went to visit my grandmother at Bilatserkva. I played in the public gardens and it was in these same gardens that one day they gathered children from infants to seven years old and shot them."

Andrej meticulously scoured the German archives. He often went to Ludwigsburg where he gathered testimonies, decades-old affidavits from the policemen who had participated in the executions. He sorted and translated them, thereby providing us with a very rich documentation that allowed us to prepare and better understand each trip. It was also he who, before each departure, located the extermination sites, estimated the number of victims, and determined the date of the events according to the German and Soviet archives, and the work of historians.

Patrice Bensimon was also part of the team. He lived in Paris and was finishing his doctorate on the places of Jewish memory in Ukraine and Belorussia. He bore the name of a Sephardic family and spoke Russian, Ukrainian, and Yiddish fluently: a rare bird. It was he who translated all the Russian testimonies into French, and who acted as our interpreter in Ukraine.

In addition, there were all those who every evening transcribed the day's interviews. It was a thankless task. During the whole trip, at night, having listened to six or seven shepherds and farm laborers recounting the assassination of their neighbors during the day, they spent half the night writing, so that we would remember. Without these transcripts we would never have known where we were because, unconsciously, the whole team tried, the following day, to forget everything we had heard the day before. Among those who helped with this task were Jean-François Bodin, head of communications at Radio Chrétiennes Francophones, and Pierre-Philippe Preux, a geography and history teacher, both passionate about contemporary history.

And then there were the drivers: Vassili, Ivan, and Eugene. They agreed to take us along the most difficult routes, despite ditches to cross, heavy snow, and the fog . . .

I was surrounded by a team of competent people who knew how to make a film, draw up historical notes, drive a truck, and find bullets.

Beyond these skills there are paths, encounters, and ties that are formed but little spoken of, perhaps out of modesty or respect for each individual's very private suffering. Between us there was also the link of faith, faith in God for some, and for others the conviction that at the heart of our quest was a sacred purpose that we must fulfill, together.

VII

DISCOVERING THE TRUTH

If our research took us from village to village, and from region to region, it also led us from discovery to discovery. Gradually, as we met people and heard their testimonies, I accepted this knowledge, bit by bit, though not without a certain apprehension.

May 9, 2005, Paris, late at night.
Sleep does not come. I watched a documentary on a woman who is looking for mass graves in Bosnia. In that country, corpses were scattered by the assassins, who deliberately dug up the bodies of the Bosnians who had been shot, and dismembered them so that their families could not identify them. This woman was working to put the bodies back together so that they could be given a decent burial. She combed the forest with her team, all of whom were wearing large white bags on their back in which to pick up the scattered body parts. Suddenly she

appeared alone on the screen with a metal detector in the middle of bushes. The journalist asked her: "Why a metal detector?" She replied, very sure of herself," "Where there are cartridges, there are bodies."

I didn't sleep that night. Had the Germans left behind their cartridges? I immersed myself in German and Soviet archives to find out. I questioned specialists and watched tapes of living witnesses. I could find no trace that Germans had collected their spent cartridges. No mention of bags or wooden cases in which they were put. In a glimmer of hope, I felt sure that the cartridges existed and that they were still buried in the Ukrainian soil. I knew that where there was a cartridge, an execution had taken place.

On my return to Ukraine I was possessed by a single obsession: to find those spent cartridges. I called on Micha to help me.

The first time I took him with me to track down cartridges, it was in Khvativ. I was a little skeptical. Micha walked round with a metal detector, making large circles of about a 300–meter radius around what we knew must have been the place of execution. Then these circles decreased until he reached the place where the shooter had stood. I quickly got used to the sound of the detector, waiting for its background noise to change into a signal. Without understanding his way of working, I left him to it. Suddenly, Micha stopped and started lifting the earth with his spade. He leaned down and picked up a little object as one would pick up a mushroom. He turned toward me and lifting his hand, he said in a loud voice: "*Niemetska Ghilse!*" Svetlana looked at me, surprised, and translated: "A German cartridge." I ran over. Micha was indeed holding between his fingers a spent cartridge covered in soil.

"How do you know it's a German cartridge?" I asked him.

"Look," he explained. "A Russian cartridge has a very wide base but not German ones. German ones also have a manufacturing mark." As he was speaking, he grabbed hold of a cloth and rubbed the base of the cartridge. One could see a mark and date of manufacture: 1938. The circles began again, of 300, 350, and then 200 meters. The dance went on for hours. Three hundred times I heard: "*Niemetska Ghilse!*"

As for me, I waited, leaning against a tree, soaked under a rain that fell relentlessly through the branches. Despite everything and despite myself, my eyes and my tired mind darted between the bones spread across the earth where marauders had dug, and the German cartridges strewn over the ground, further away on my left. Micha had been piling them up on a piece of newspaper. When he found the 300th cartridge, I asked him to stop for a while. I was filled with revulsion and discomfort: "A bullet, a Jew. A Jew, a cartridge."[1] The Germans did not use more than one bullet to kill a Jew. Three hundred cartridges, 300 bullets, 300 people executed here. My sense of unease did not go away. No Russian cartridge. The proof of genocide was so flagrant and so real. There was no longer a distance or a barrier between me and the reality. I was faced with the evidence of the horror, leaning against a tree, freezing cold under a rain that formed little rivulets on the ground.

We took a break of 20 or 25 minutes. No one spoke. Micha began again, explaining to me that at a certain period the Germans had no more good metal to make the cartridges, and that is why there was a difference in the amount of damage in the ones we were finding. From the position of the spent cartridges, we could identify the position of the shooters, who were standing not far from the pit for their successive shootings. When they had finished, they had covered the cartridges with a bit of earth: we were finding them at different depths separated by a little mud. We had to dig deeper, as trees had grown, and cartridges had lodged among their roots. With each new discovery, we recorded distances between the pits and the spent cartridges using the GPS (Global Positioning System).

It was late and we had to go back. In the morning, discreetly, Micha had asked me how Jews were buried . . . usually. I saw him move off and place, one by one, the scattered bones that had been thrown into the open hole of the plundered pit, cover them with earth, place a stone and then, in silence, cut several green branches, and make a *Magen David* (Star of David) on the grave. We all stood still as though time were suspended. Tears came to my eyes with the feeling that I had, at my humble level, helped reestablish dignity for these Jewish women and men who had been shot here one day in the summer of 1942, summarily buried, and then desecrated.

As we had no bag in which to gather the cartridges, we used our pullovers and pockets. We went down the hill, loaded with our discoveries. Micha took us to a restaurant; we went upstairs, and he greeted the waitresses, whom he seemed to know, then put a chair across the door to block it and said to us: "Now we must count them." We emptied our pullovers in the middle of a large wooden table in a badly lit room under a swinging pale light. We placed the cartridges in rows like police booty, and sorted them according to whether they were exploded cartridges, made from better metal, cartridges for heavy machine guns, or machine gun rifles. I will never forget the memory of counting the cartridges of the assassination of Jews in a small village in Ukrainian Galicia.

That day in the restaurant we counted 600 cartridges. Guillaume got up on the table to photograph them from above. I understood that we had to record all these traces, the traces of the assassinations, and collect all these cartridges that constituted the proof of this Shoah by bullets. No gas chambers, no automation, no so-called "mechanization." A man assassinating another man. In the archives, we discovered other traces: records of German battalions of which each member had been obliged to kill at least one Jew. Everyone had to be implicated, so that no one could say: "I didn't kill a Jew." It is recorded that Paul Blobel, the man who had coordinated the executions in Kiev, had obliged his driver, who had not wanted to kill, to assassinate several Jews. One day, Blobel had him stop the car and told him to kill some. The driver had gotten out of the car, and shot, once, ten times, and more for several long minutes. When Blobel had decided that his driver had killed enough, they got back in the car and left.[2]

With the cartridges, we also found hundreds of rusted, empty cartridge clips. Most of them were clips for Mauser rifles that could contain five bullets. That explained why the Nazis had made Jewish families come forward in groups of five people. Many witnesses subsequently told us that they had seen the assassins reload their rifle between two families. Micha also found other objects: a rather dented metallic aluminum goblet, apparently lost by a German; the metal frame of a Walther pistol, rusty and almost fossilized; little metal chains used to clean the shaft of machine guns when they overheated; and some handles of cartridge boxes.

Micha always had with him a catalog describing the equipment used by the units of the Reich during World War II. We also found the metal hoops of a barrel. A rather elderly shepherd came to see us with his brown and white dog while we were looking for cartridges and told us that at the end of a killing, one of the Germans had placed a barrel of quicklime over the bodies on a plank laid across the pit. He then shot at the barrel to make it explode. The peasant added that the German had asked them to bring him water so that he could wash his hands at the end of the execution of the Jews. When he had rinsed them, he had thrown the basin behind his back as if to say "I wash my hands of this."

Several months earlier we had searched this same place in the forest for two hours with two elderly villagers without finding anything. One of them had had trouble walking but had absolutely wanted to uncover the place. With his wooden cane, he had poked into the brambles, muttering, "It's a long time since I was here. It has changed a lot . . . I think that it was here . . . no, over there . . ." They had the greatest difficulty in orienting themselves, but they were driven by a certainty: the Jews had been killed here. Since World War II, the forest had been known throughout the region as the *Lis na jevrjejakh,* the "Forest over the Jews." We finally had gotten tired of circling in vain around such a large forest and had decided to stop our search for the day. To take the witnesses back home we used what they called the "white route," a chalky route that had been eroded by water and which left a white deposit on our clothes.

Throughout my search, in village after village, I heard the same declarations: "Down there, there are no more inhabitants in the village," or "Jewish kolkhozes in our region? They have completely disappeared," or "There are no more old people in our area, they have all died," or "We aren't from here, we are all from elsewhere, we were deported from Poland," or also "This is a new area and no one was here during the war." These hasty responses only increased my determination. When I heard them, I knew that I had to carry on looking, and I knew that I would find what I was looking for.

After an hour and a half of walking, we entered the village of Khvativ. At the entrance to the village was a farm. A woman of 40 or so was standing leaning on her blue gate. I asked her: "Are there elderly people in your village?" The answer I had so often heard before came: "No." My interpreter turned to me: "You see, Patrick, in this village there are no elderly people." This was beginning to irritate me. "Yes, I know, in this country there are no elderly people." I continued on my way and asked the same question of a passer-by. He indicated a house where, he said, someone aged 91 lived. A breakthrough! Svetlana pushed the little wooden gate held back by a metal latch. She crossed the yard, climbed three steps up to the porch, and then disappeared into the house. She only reappeared half an hour later, her head lowered, disillusioned: "She saw everything but she doesn't want to talk. She is frightened of the KGB." The whole team got ready to go, disappointed. But I could not bring myself to leave the village, and I continued watching the house. How could I go when there was someone inside who knew everything? I would not leave. I waited, standing against the closed gate, watching the door like a supplicant.

After 45 minutes, the door of the house edged, very gently, open. An old woman, small and a little bent, leaning on a stick of knotted wood, came out. She was wearing a grey anorak and a lovely blue scarf. She came over slowly, lifted her eyes up to me, and sat down silently on a bench. Her name was Olena, and she was willing to talk. After making sure she was not about to leave again, I went to fetch Svetlana, so that she could translate the old lady's words for me. My team settled in and she began.

She was a young bride on the day of the Jews' execution. She was bringing in the harvest on top of the white mountain with a female friend; the wheat was ripe, and the weather was hot. In the far distance they caught sight of two German military trucks, filled with Jewish women, standing up. The trucks approached until they passed them. In one of the trucks she suddenly recognized a friend of her mother's who began shouting "Olena, Olena, save me!" She paused for breath. "The more she shouted, the more I hid myself in the wheat. I was young, and I was afraid that the Germans would kill us like they were killing the Jews. That woman shouted until they took her to the pit. Right until the last moment I heard her shouting: "Olena, Olena, save me!" These words punctuated her tale again and again. It was the first time a witness had communicated to us the last words of a Jewish person executed by the Nazis.

We sat there on the blue wooden bench for a long time, in silence, contemplating together the landscape of our painful memories. After having seen her talking to us, several neighbors come to reproach her. She replied only: "You know, at my age I am not frightened of anything any more, not even death!" I saw Olena again, several times. Thanks to her we found the exact location of the mass graves in the "Forest over the Jews." With this interview I discovered that the witnesses knew the victims by name, but that they could do nothing.

Khvativ, Olena's testimony, and the discovery of the cartridges provided us with complementary proofs of this genocide. From then on, we tried to find all the cartridges for all the mass graves we visited, as palpable proof of the massacre. We obtained a more powerful metal detector. We wanted to find proof of the executions without opening the graves, and we wanted to identify the position of the shooters. I learned how to recognize German cartridges as well as all types of German weapons: Walther pistols through Mauser rifles—these were the most-used weapon—as well as machine gun pistols, and heavy machine guns. Also, in the middle of their testimonies, the villagers imitated the sound of the shots. They had never forgotten the "tac, silence, tac" of a Mauser rifle, or the "tac, tac, tac, tac" of a machine gun pistol.

Micha also taught us how to recognize bones. One day, we found a dog who had made his home in the middle of the unearthed bones in a pit. Micha showed us the difference between a human bone and an animal one, unfortunately quite easy to recognize. Here the last trace of human and religious dignity was lost: the burial of the bones of one's dead. Men, women, and children without tombs or burial place appeared to us as the supreme token of dehumanization.

That landscape became the backdrop to death. I will never forget Khvativ and its "Forest over the Jews," Olena and her blue eyes that have seen so much, the cartridges, and all those small objects thrown away by the assassins who believed they were acting with total impunity. And that voice, that cry that had resonated through the forest, those last words: "Olena, Olena, save me!"

In Khvativ, I understood that we had to depart from our empirical method. Coalescence of proof that the executions took place became an absolute necessity. That obliged us to create a new work method. As Mrs. Revcolevschi, director of the Foundation for the Memory of the Shoah, often repeated, "the work is characterized by its rigor"—in other words, we could no longer simply visit the villages where the Jews had lived—we had the duty to visit all the villages in Ukraine, search the Soviet, East-German, and West-German archives, and use ballistic research, as well as enquiries on the ground: the testimonies.

VIII

ACCEPTING THE TRUTH

In my experience, the most difficult part of discovering and gaining personal knowledge of genocide is accepting the truth about what happened. To know all the details while at the same time being able to continue to live a full life, without forgetting or hiding what one knows about the past.

It is no longer a question of getting stuck with certain impressions, of feeling sick, or worse, of remaining immobilized with terror. Terror is part of the strategy of those who commit genocide. Like predators, they create ways of petrifying their victims before killing them. When the Jewish victims got off the trains onto the *Judenrampe,* between Auschwitz and Birkenau, they were terrified. When the family of a kolkhoze Jew was suddenly taken to the edge of an irrigation well 70 meters deep to be thrown into it, they were paralyzed with fear. Terror can be generated by the sole mention of genocide, by the reading of a book on the subject, or at seeing archival images of it, or on visiting a former concentration camp. If, sixty years later, we allow ourselves to be terrified as well, though, we are allowing the people of the Third Reich, who perpetrated genocide, an additional victory. Terror can immobilize thought and awareness, and hinder the ability to remain responsible, confrontational, and strong in front of the perpetrators of genocide.

These perpetrators are like serial killers, only they operate on a much larger scale, at a national or continental level. They certainly are not terrified, and they know that most people cannot and do not want to think of the possibility of an act of genocide. Ordinary people want to sleep, and the simple thought of genocide can prevent an ordinary person from sleeping. The perpetrators of genocide bank on this to set up mechanisms for mass killing in all tranquility: No one will be able to conceive, hence accept and want to believe, the truth.

How many people warned the public that genocide was taking place back in 1941? How many times were they disappointed by others' incredulity in response to this information? When Gerhardt Riegner[1] first received information revealing the extent of the intended genocide of the Jews, did he not take some time before reacting, since that information seemed unthinkable to him? The unbelievable nature of genocide is a weapon often used by those who perform it, whether it is the genocide of the Jews, the Armenians, or the Tutsis in Rwanda, and allows the perpetrators to deny their feat. This common incapacity to accept genocide is known by those who commit it and to their accomplices; it is built into their plans. That is perhaps why genocides are perpetrated without concern for discretion. Mass assassins know that the witnesses will be heard but seldom believed.

The other weapon used by people who commit genocide is lack of compassion. I am convinced that when genocide is taking place, many people can sleep easily at night—if they are sure that they will not be killed.

The perpetrators of genocide know each other and gain strength from one another. Did Hitler not cite, several times, the genocide of the Armenians? In his speech to the commanders in chief of the German army on August 22, 1939, Hitler is reported to have said: "Who remembers the genocide of the Armenians today?"[2]

Accepting awareness of what happened—men individually and personally murdering a child, a grandmother, a couple in the open street, in the marketplace, behind the church, in a ditch—is to help new generations become resistant to genocide mechanisms which could be set in motion, again, anywhere in the world.

Why did I continue to visit villages and houses in Ukraine, one after the other, combing the roads for the smallest hamlet where a Jew was murdered, just as the Germans had done 60 years ago? I did it because genocides are multiplying and reproducing themselves. Because, since the Shoah, there have been other genocides. As the French philosopher Simone Weil has stated: "And yet, the vow that we have all so often expressed of 'never again' has not been fulfilled, because other genocides have been perpetrated. We, the survivors, have the right and even the duty to warn you and ask you that 'never again' becomes a reality."

I have often heard the comment: "We have spent enough time on the victims; now we need to spend time on the assassins." How could I take on such a point of view? Even if it is legitimate, of course, to study the assassins and their collaborators, I feel we still need to study the victims with empathy to fully understand the Shoah. Studying the Shoah from the point of view of the assassins could be undermined by a fascination for "absolute" evil and the sadistic voyeurism that often accompanies it.

Cardinal Lustiger has explained that the perpetrator of genocide—the mass assassin—has to abolish a law—the law against killing—to carry out his terrible project. Hitler had the malign intuition of the close link between the commandment, "Thou shalt not kill," and the Jewish people: to abolish this injunction he decided to exterminate the people who had received it on Mount Sinai. The Final Solution and the abolition of the sanctions against murder were irrevocably linked. Seen in this light, the genocide of the Jews becomes the prototype of all genocides. To study and teach the Shoah does not eliminate the need to understand the mass murderers but must enable us to understand the phenomenon in depth, and to create a consciousness that is resistant to all future possible attempts at genocide.

Yet, accepting knowledge about the Shoah in Eastern Europe is a difficult path. Some gave up, unable to bear that knowledge brutally imposed upon us.

In order not to know, our mind might cling to preconceptions which, as by a sleight of hand, make uncomfortable bits of reality disappear. I was not immune to such a process. Only time has allowed me to get past the clichés and reality to impose itself, little by little, over my mind.

During my first searches, for example, I was convinced that all the mass graves were hidden in the forests. I had always been told that the Jews had been murdered in secret in the middle of the woods, far from view. In other words, I had the greatest difficulty accepting that they had been killed in the middle of the village and believing the veracity of the testimonies I was gathering.

The first witness who took us to a mass grave located at the center of a village was a man named Vassil Protski. A short man, wearing a blue cap, he took us to an area of individual houses and went over to the edge of a wide lawn. He said: "This is where they were killed. I was watching from down there, at the side of the road, 20 meters away." The owners of several neighboring houses came running out—apparently they had understood what we were talking about. One of them interrupted the witness: "My vegetable allotment patch. That's my vegetable patch! Leave our gardens alone." Without realizing it, with their protestations they were only confirming what everyone in the area knew: the bodies of shot Jews were resting under the tomato plants.

So I discovered that the Jews had not all been killed in forests. The Nazis feared the forests because often they concealed groups of resistance fighters—Soviet partisans. Thus the Germans assassinated the Jews in the middle of towns, in full view and with the knowledge of everyone.

These peasants also spoke to me of the pits as if they were alive. How was I to understand what they meant? How was I to accept the witnesses' repeated assertion that the pits "breathed" for three days afterward? I attributed it, without yet having explained it, to the deterioration process of the bodies. And then, on a different day in another village, someone who had been requisitioned as a child to dig that pit told us that a hand coming out of the ground had grabbed hold of his spade. I understood then that all the witnesses who had told us about the pits moving, accompanying their words by an up and down movement of the hand, had signified in fact that a pit took three days to quiet down because many of the victims had been buried alive. After understanding that, I accepted the true meaning of these words: "The pit took three days to die . . ." "The well shouted for three days." Some victims were only wounded or even had been thrown alive into the pits. Those who did not fall were pushed in. Assistants had given a helping hand to those who did not fall. The victims suffocated in the two or three meters of sand that was thrown on top of them.

It was the same difficult process for each new discovery. One I found particularly difficult to grasp was the requisitions of villagers. I was astonished the first time a witness told me that he had seen an execution, but that feeling paled in comparison to how I felt when I understood what really happened. Martin Grygrory Petrovitch was an old man. He and his wife had come to open the door for us; both very thin and very tall. They wanted to talk to us. We sat down on a bench and the old man told me he had been requisitioned to dig a pit and then to cover it. He had tried to refuse to guard the Jews, but the Germans had forced him to sit down on top of the pit. We went with him to the site of the pit. He repeated his story. Until that moment, we had not known that civilians had been requisitioned to dig the pits. From then on we dared ask the question: "Who dug the pits?"

The same process occurred with most of the questions that I asked the witnesses. As my knowledge and understanding grew, I began asking questions that I would have never dared asking before, such as "Who pulled out the teeth?" I started asking that after I discovered that people were given bags and pincers to pull out the Jews' gold teeth. A woman of 91, Anna Tchouprina, began crying during a very long testimony given from her bed, as she had remembered the death of Jewish children; she repeated over and over, "It's not possible, it's not possible . . ." They had killed more than 8,000 people in view of her house. One day, one of her sons, a teenager, had come back to the house with his back red with blood. The Germans had beaten him: "They wanted him to pull teeth out but he didn't want to so they beat him." I asked her: "How did they pull out the teeth?" She replied, "With pincers!" From then on I would ask in the most natural manner: "Who pulled the teeth out? Where were they put?"

In another region, the Nazis encouraged the Romanians to kill the Jews because they had typhus. The Germans requisitioned teenagers to bring hemp and sunflowers with which to burn the corpses. I had to first accept that fact in order to be able to ask: "Did you find the sunflowers in a factory or a field? Who grew hemp in the village?" And it was in this way, bit by bit, truth after truth, discomfort after discomfort, discovery after discovery, that I was able to reconstitute the exact landscape of the horror.

What enabled me to go on was forcing myself not to judge the person who was speaking to me, as I kept making more and more surprising and horrid discoveries. We found out that the Germans had had carte blanche regarding how to kill the Jews. A legal framework was in place that required them to assassinate the Jews, but the methods used were left to their initiative, even their sadism.

With the influence of my family and my religious tradition, I have always taken the position of resistance in the face of evil—I am a person who unites with others to fight evil wherever it resides, knowing that one can sometimes be influenced and become its actor or instigator. I think my upbringing and education is what allows me to hold on. I am convinced that there is only one human race—a human race that shoots two-year-old children. For better or for worse I belong to that human race and this allows me to acknowledge that an ideology can deceive minds to the point of annihilating all ethical reflexes and all recognition of the human in the other.

It happened in 1941, 1942, 1943, and 1944, in the very heart of Europe, one of the oldest civilizations in the world that had been shaped by centuries of Christian religious thinking and by the Enlightenment—yet human beings had stopped recognizing their own fellows! Human beings had not seen that by killing others, they were killing themselves. This enigma, this non-recognition of human by human, has always preoccupied me. It was one of the enigmas that provoked my faith: the human being is created in the image of God but is never completely capable of recognizing another human, to the extent that, in the worst circumstances, he can murder the other. The more I studied the genocide of the Jews and the behavior of the Nazis, of the collaborators, of the curious onlookers, of the passive, and of those who were assassinated for no reason, the more I realized that believing in the human race is a serious responsibility, and a position that needs to be consciously created and constructed. It is not enough to affirm or declare the truth; one must really commit oneself to the endeavor of developing a deep conscience, because, clearly from my own experience, a conscience is a fragile entity. There are photos that show the German assassins taking a break before killing the last Jews. One can make out the faces of these young men, in their early twenties, who are nothing out of the ordinary—human beings killing other human beings without realizing that they too are men.

Olena S., Vorokhta, Ivano-Frankivsk region, Galicia, August 20, 2005
Olena did not want to talk in front of the other villagers. She arranged to meet us in the woods an hour and a half later. We saw her arriving with a cow, explaining that she hadn't found anyone to look after it. She was very frightened. Before leaving, she made us promise not to reveal her surname.

Patrick Desbois: What year were you born?
Olena S.: In 1932.
P.D.: Where did you live during the war?
O.S.: Here.

P.D.: What happened in this forest?

O.S.: Nothing. Cows grazed here. I was here. Oh! . . . During the war . . . Nothing happened.

P.D.: What happened between the Germans and the Jews in this forest?

O.S.: The Germans killed the Jews.

P.D.: Did you come here when it took place? Before or after the shooting?

O.S: Yes. I saw them dig the pit and bring the Jews, that's all.

P.D.: How many people dug the pits?

O.S.: Four. They dug a large pit in the morning and in the evening a big truck arrived with Jews and Germans with rifles. And the shootings began. They killed them, and then they covered up the pit.

P.D.: How long did they take to dig the pit?

O.S.: Perhaps five hours. They killed the Jews in the evening. The same four people came to dig the pit the next day.

P.D.: For how many days did they dig the pits?

O.S.: I don't know. But in the evening the truck left again . . . Oh! How many times . . . I don't know. They arrived in the morning, dug, brought them and killed them in the evening, and so on . . . They dug one and then filled it. The next day, they dug another.

P.D.: Were the Jews brought in a truck?

O.S.: Yes, a very big one. They were lying down, covered with cloth. They opened the truck. Then they put a plank over the pit, the Jews moved onto the plank, they were shot in the back and in the nape of the neck and they fell . . . One young woman was very beautiful.

P.D.: Did the Germans make them undress?

O.S.: Yes.

P.D.: Completely?

O.S.: I don't know. It was covered up and no one reopened it, but it was still moving.

P.D.: Did the earth move because some of them were not dead?

O.S.: I didn't see it myself; people told me that.

P.D.: Were the clothes distributed to the people who dug the ditches?

O.S.: I don't know. Perhaps.

P.D.: Were there babies and children?

O.S.: There were people of all ages. When they searched the pit, they found little bones and little shoes. There were also adult bones. They dug, made piles and then put everything back in the pit. It was in the 1950s or 1960s. I don't remember. I came to see it being dug up.

P.D.: Did they bring the bodies out one after the other?

O.S.: They weren't whole bodies. There were little pieces of bone, the color of wheat, and the remains of a person who must have been fat. There were skulls and pieces of bone.

P.D.: Were there Jews who were killed in town, before being put into the trucks, and brought here?

O.S.: They were all alive. No one could get out or jump from the truck. One man managed to get out of the pit; he went to ask for help at a neighboring house and the villager accompanied him to the border. At the end of the war this Jew went to Rakhiv; he had a very long beard. He recognized the person who had saved him and tapped him on the shoulder asking him "Do you recognize me?" The other replied no and he said to him: "You saved my life." And he gave him money. Not much, of course, because it wasn't long after the war.

P.D.: And so none of the people who were only wounded got out of the pit?

O.S.: No, just that one person. In most cases, they shot them in the head.

IX

THEY SAW

The witnesses who lived near the sites of the executions before and during the war still live there today. I remember the woman who said to me, sincerely bewildered: "I don't know why they killed them in front of my house . . ." She was spending the remaining months of her life at home, in a room with a window overlooking the mass grave. The lives of these people, battered by Soviet history, had been suddenly crossed by the Shoah. One day Germans had arrived in their village; destroying everything in their path, they had taken the Jews and shot them.

The witnesses who spoke to us are simple people who had not been swallowed up by the Soviet system, because they were too poor. Peasants who keep a cow tied on a rope, exactly as they did 60 years ago. Beggars or farm workers who bring in the harvest. People whose path, or that of their animals, had happened to cross the path that led to the extermination of the Jews. When we asked them if people had come to the village since the war to talk to them, they told us: "No, you are the first." When, before ending an interview, I would ask them why they had never spoken, they all responded that they had never been asked. These are people who saw what happened but who could do nothing. Powerless people who still ask themselves whether they are guilty or innocent, when they were only six, seven, eight, or nine years old at the time these events occurred. These children who ran behind the lines of Jews who were throwing away their last possessions—necklaces, wedding rings, and the few bits of jewelry they had left—so as not to leave them to the Germans. These curious children who ran along behind the Jews, up to the place of execution, hiding in the grass or climbing up into the trees to watch. These children who saw their fathers dig the pits and their classmates stripped naked before being shot.

Today, these children are now in their seventies and they want to talk. Some of them are broken by what they saw and experienced. I remember one man, Samuel Arabski, who had been watching from behind a bush when he was requisitioned to fill in the pit. Now an old man, he explained to us, his eyes still full of terror, that a Jew's hand had emerged from the pit and seized his spade. He had fainted. The pit was covered but "it was moving all over."

The witnesses we questioned fell into three categories.

There were indirect witnesses, people who did not see the assassinations but who had heard about them or had seen the Jews leaving town. They told us how, for example, they had seen the police taking the Jews from their homes and had watched them disappear from the corner of the street.

Then there were the direct witnesses, who had been present at the assassination. Like Yaroslav Galan, who told us that he had seen several trucks arrive while he was tending a cow. Thirty or so people had gotten out of these trucks. He saw them digging and then being shot. He heard the orders of the Germans and the last words of the Jews. This second group constituted the majority of our witnesses.

And then there were others: civilians, mostly children, who had been requisitioned for a day or a week. A local policeman, an emissary from the mayor, or a German officer would go into people's houses and order: "You come with me and bring a spade." They could be requisitioned to dig a pit at 5 in the morning. After they had finished digging, the Germans made them sit down while they brought in the Jews and shot them, and then they had them get up and fill in the pit. Some were assigned the task of gathering up the clothes, passing by with a cart so the Jews should put their clothes into it. When the cart was full, they took it to a house designated by the Germans to store the loot. Others were requisitioned to pull out teeth. Still others to transport the Jews in their carts when the pit was too far from the village and there weren't enough trucks. Most of them were forced to act at gunpoint. They had no choice.

It took me years to understand the scope of these requisitions.

Nikolaï Olkhusky, Konstiantynivka, Zaporijie region, December 31, 2006

Nikolaï was 11 at the time of the events. As a child he was present at the assassination of all the columns of Jews whom he saw being brought and shot.

Patrick Desbois: Where did you live during the war?
Nikolaï Olkhusky: I lived here. There is my old house, down there.
P.D.: What did the Germans do here?

N.O.: They immediately brought the Jews, for two or three days. They had gathered them in the town of Melitopol. They brought them from the town to here, on foot, in four columns. And they shot them down there in the anti-tank ditch.

P.D.: How long did it take a column to arrive?

N.O.: The column was endless. They walked and walked from the town until they got to where they were shot. There were four rows.

P.D.: Were the people in the column adults or children?

N.O.: There were people of every age—children, old people. They had been told to gather because they were going to be taken to work somewhere and that they should take some food and their children because there would be nurseries in which they would be looked after . . . The Jews had a sort of red armband. Then they were told to undress and they were thrown into the pits. At the end of the day I went to look; the earth was moving.

P.D.: Were the gunmen already in place before the column arrived?

N.O.: Yes. They were already there with submachine guns and machine guns.

P.D.: How did the Germans arrive?

N.O.: They came in trucks, which arrived, waited, and left again. There were four or five trucks.

P.D.: Were there many gunmen?

N.O.: Yes, 20 or so. I didn't count them.

P.D.: Did they all shoot at the same time or did they take turns?

N.O.: They all shot at the same time. They were on one side of the ditch, they made people come forward and they shot them. The ditch was steep on one side and less steep on the other side. On the sloping side were the soldiers. There was another soldier behind, next to the place where people undressed so that they could not escape. They didn't make them wait. They made them undress quickly and move to the edge of the ditch. Some of them were entirely naked, others in a shirt . . .

P.D.: Who made them move to the edge of the ditch?

N.O.: Germans and also policemen. They treated them badly, kicking them so they wouldn't escape.

P.D.: Were children also shot?

N.O.: Yes. Perhaps the ones who were in their parents' arms fell into the ditch alive. As I said, the earth was still moving afterwards.

P.D.: How long did the shooting last when there was a long column?

N.O.: Four or five hours.

P.D.: Were you hiding in the grass when you saw this or did you see it from your house?

N.O.: I was grazing my cow.

P.D.: Do you think the Jews knew they were going to be killed?

N.O.: No, the people at the head of the column didn't know. They realized when they arrived at the ditch. Me too, I was almost shot. I had approached to see the shooting and a German saw me, caught hold of me and made me join them. Luckily, there was a Russian who had been requisitioned to cover the ditches and he told them: "No, he's a Russian." They chased me away and I went to one side where I could observe everything.

P.D.: Did some Jews try to escape?

N.O.: Some tried but they didn't get very far from the pit because they were shot very quickly.

P.D.: Were they shot in the pit or above it?

N.O.: They were shot in the pit itself. They made them climb down into it and then they shot them directly in the pit, then threw earth on top of the bodies. The pit was very long.

P.D.: Were the columns composed just of Jews?

N.O.: Yes, there weren't any Russians in that column. The partisans were taken in a truck a bit further on when all the Jews had been killed.

P.D.: Did the Germans leave immediately after the executions?

N.O.: The Germans shot people and then left. The police and the requisitioned Russians stayed to cover up the grave.

P.D.: Were the Russians requisitioned in the morning?

N.O.: They began shooting in the morning and by around 1 or 2 pm, everything was already finished. Then they filled in the ditch but they didn't put much earth on top. Dogs came to rummage and pull things out. Then you could see the bodies.

P.D.: Were the clothes taken away?

N.O.: They took some away and the requisitioned Russians took some as well. Many people took them. The clothes were in a heap and people were allowed to take them.

P.D.: Were there Jews who came out of the pit alive because they were only wounded?

N.O.: I cannot tell you. I wasn't next to the pit.

P.D.: Did you tell your parents what had happened?

N.O.: Yes. They scolded me, saying: "Why did you go poke around down there?"

P.D.: In your opinion, how many mass executions were there?

N.O.: There was only one mass execution, during a single day. After that they brought several people in a truck. Such a big column of people happened only once. After the big shooting, they brought gypsies, Jews, and partisans and shot them. But they weren't mass shootings. One or two trucks came and they shot them. They didn't undress them; the trucks stopped at the edge of the ditch, they threw them in the ditch and then shot them.

P.D.: **Is that pit with the great mass of people next to the monument?**

N.O.: No. The monument is over there, while the people were shot over there, behind our area, at the end of the village.

P.D.: **Could you show us that place?**

N.O.: I could show you roughly where it is because the ditch has been filled in since then.

P.D.: **In your opinion, why did the Germans kill the Jews like that?**

N.O.: Who knows? Hitler didn't like the Jews; they shot them everywhere, not just here. I don't know why he didn't like them.

P.D.: **Thank you very much. Would you agree to your testimony being put in the archives and in museums?**

N.O.: Of course. I have told you all that I know.

X

THE REQUISITIONS

Every village is a different crime scene. Every case is particular.

Genocide was regulated by law, but commando heads were given free rein in terms of how to carry it out. The way the massacres took place depended on the circumstances—topography, the presence of partisans—different factors that the Germans had to weigh to perpetrate the most rapid and efficient assassinations possible.

Those who taught me the most about the shooting of the Jews were, without any doubt, the people who had been "requisitioned."

I distinctly remember the first time a witness told me that he had been requisitioned during the Nazis' assassination of the Jews. The surprise was two-fold: first of all, at the role these people played, and secondly at the fact that they were still alive.

The Germans did not kill the requisitioned once they had done their work, for fear that their murder would be discovered. These "requisitioned" were not Ukrainian police, collaborators, or even sympathizers, but mostly young men, women, children, or adolescents who, for one or two days, had been requisitioned from their homes, early in the morning, by a man with a gun. The requisitioned were not watching the columns of Jews marching to the pits from their windows. Neither were they watching perched up in an oak tree or hidden behind a bush. They were at the site of the crime, very often before the Jews arrived. They were present, from beginning to end, at the shootings, beside the Jews and their assassins, sometimes sitting in the grass only a few meters away from them.

All the requisitioned I met spoke of the infamy with which, for one day or for several hours, and against their will, they had been associated. Not only were they present at the event, but they had also been forced to participate—with their spade, their cart, their bag, their saucepan, their sewing needle, or their tambourine, depending on the task imposed on them by the Germans. Every testimony of someone who had been requisitioned plunged us further into the horror of the murder of the Jews and the everyday reality of the Holocaust by bullets.

The first person I met who had been requisitioned said he had arrived after the execution of the Jews to clean the site. He told us that the Germans had made them come after the shootings, bringing chlorine and ash to stop the blood from running out of the pits. From these first meetings, I learned, by listening to the witnesses, that the assassins prepared these killing sprees by seeking out "personnel" the day before or at the break of day. The requisitions did not happen spontaneously but were part of the careful preparation for the implementation of their crimes. Sometimes more than 150 children were put to their service. Forced to participate, these children saw everything. Today, they are like windows through which we can see and understand.

My memory of each one of them remains vivid.

The "presser," Ternivka, July 23, 2007

The archives state that 2,300 Jews were killed in this little village. Since we started looking for witnesses in the morning, numerous villagers, who say they were not present the day of the assassinations, tell us about a certain Petrivna who "saw everything."

I am usually distrustful of this kind of information, as the someone who is supposed to know, most of the time, saw nothing. I found that in Ukraine, when someone directs you to somebody else it usually means: "I didn't see anything! Go back to where you came from!"

By evening, as I had met no reliable witness, I resolved to look for Petrivna after all. We embarked again on the road we had already taken countless times, a rough path winding between the houses in the village. The sun was already low. Svetlana, weary at the end of this unproductive day, opened the sliding door of the van without enthusiasm and jumped down with a thud. Several minutes later, she came out of the house making expansive gestures with her hands. "The lady saw everything," she cried.

Petrivna was sitting in her courtyard with two friends, on a little wooden bench against the white cement wall. Her tale began very peacefully, without apparent emotion: "A 'punitive' German commando came into the village to kill the Jews, under the responsibility of the head of the local Gestapo, a certain Hummel. They were gathered in the main street in front of Hummel's house and then arranged in columns of four across. The Jewish children and the handicapped were torn from their families and placed in horse-drawn carts that were following the columns." From her house, she gestured far into the distance with her hand toward the center of the village, indicating the gathering-point. "The columns of Jews were taken toward a great pit just outside the village. The German gunmen were placed above the pit. The Jews went down into the pit, twenty by twenty." The assassins used the so-called Jeckeln method;[1] The Jews had to walk down into the pit—a slope had been prepared for this on one side—and they then had to lie down on the bodies of their dead comrades before being assassinated by a bullet in the head or in the nape of the neck.

Suddenly, Petrivna stopped talking, her body twitching bizarrely. She said in a single breath, her hands moving up and down: "You see, it's not easy to walk on bodies," trying to express that the ground was moving. In a flash, I realized she was trying to convey her unspeakable experience, her suffering. Very calmly I asked her: "You had to walk on the bodies of the people who were shot?" She replied: "Yes, I had to pack them down," making the same gesture with her arms. I thought I understood: "You had to do that at the end of the shootings, in the evening, or between each volley of shots?" Seeing that I was beginning to understand, she told the rest of her story. "After every volley of shots. We were three Ukrainian girls who, in our bare feet, had to pack down the bodies of the Jews and throw a fine layer of sand on top of them so that other Jews could lay down."

"Barefoot?" I asked. She replied "You know, we were very poor, we didn't have shoes. The Germans had seen me in the fields in the morning. I was tending a cow. They said to me: 'Go to your mother's house, get a spade and come back.' When I got to the house, my mother said to me: 'Go, if you don't go, they will kill you!' The other requisitioned girls were also looking after their cows. We were all poor."

I could never have imagined that the Nazis would requisition young Ukrainian girls to press the bodies down with their bare feet, as if the bodies were grapes on harvest day in wine country.

The so-called "pressers" had to put sand on the bodies so that the next Jewish victims could lie down more easily.

As I began to envision what had happened, I asked her "Did you come out of the pit between each shooting?" "Yes," she said. "The German commander gave us an order to go down into the pit and another order to come out. All together, we had to run into the pit with our spades, pack down the bodies with our feet, put down sand and then come out all together. Many Jews were only wounded . . . We had trouble walking on them."

"Did you have time to sit down between two shootings?" I asked. She answered "The shootings were so quick that we didn't even have time to catch our breath between shootings! It lasted from 10 o'clock in the morning to 4 in the afternoon. The Germans took turns to go and eat but not us." I asked "And the Jewish children?" She answered "They tore them from their mothers' arms and put them in horse-drawn carts. They were killed at the end of the main execution, after the adults. They threw them in the air. They threw them any old way."

Several times, Petrivna mentioned her Jewish classmate, who sat next to her at school. She saw her in the pit, naked. She saw her arrive and then shot, before she had to trample on her corpse. Petrivna also remembered that Hummel took two Jewish girls out of the line, a seamstress and a very pretty young woman who were to his liking. They were taken to Hummel's house and were not killed that day. At the end of the interview, Petrivna led us to the pale blue metal door with a warm smile. That evening when we got back into the van, our eyes were full of images of these three village girls running down into the pit, trampling on the bodies, throwing sand, and coming out again on the orders of Hummel, trying to catch their breath before the next shooting. All around them, Germans had been guarding the site with their dogs. The other Jews had been waiting, naked and terrified.

It was very often through a little sentence that almost seemed to slip through during a testimony, that a vital clue about the requisitioned person's experience appeared. The requisitioned would speak furtively, as though to test my listening and to find out whether I was capable of truly hearing him or her. Perhaps I missed much information during my earlier research. As I could not bear to believe, and therefore could not perceive their words, the witnesses had originally remained silent.

The way requisitions happened was different with each execution. The details seemed to be decided by the person who coordinated the assassination. The witnesses' narratives were relentlessly precise.

The seamstress, Zabolottia, July 27, 2007

Zabolottia is more like a hamlet than a village. Dirt roads, with the occasional white and grey goose running around. An old lady, quite small, was walking on the side of the road as we arrived. Our vehicle stopped beside her. "Were you here during the war?" Svetlana called out to her. Alexandra, as her name turned out to be, immediately embarked on her story, as if we had made an appointment with her.

She explained that in the middle of the village, after the execution of the Jews, the primary school had been transformed into a *Kommandantur*. She remembered that the Jews had been brought on carts, with their goods, to be killed near a lake nicknamed the sacred lake. We went there together.

It was summer, and when we arrived on the banks of the lake, a young Ukrainian couple was peacefully picnicing, grilling *chachlyki,* kebabs of marinated meat. As we approached the site of the mass grave I overheard Alexandra murmuring: "Me, I stole buttons." I turned to ask her: "Where did you steal buttons from?" She answered "I stole them from a beautiful Jewish garment." "And where was this garment?" I insisted, sensing that she was trying to say something else. She answered "In the *Kommandantur!* A German had requisitioned me with other women to work all day in the *Kommandatur,* in one of the classrooms. That is where they threw all the clothes of the murdered Jews."

Alexandra then began describing the mass of clothes that covered the floor of the classroom. The clothes had not been sorted. Her task was to patch up the best clothes so that they could be sent to Germany. "Seamstresses," I thought. The Germans requisitioned the village seamstresses after the massacres. "The needles and thread were provided by the Germans and the work had to be finished that same evening," Alexandra added.

At every stage of their operation, the Nazis made the young people of the villages work. Many ordinary people were, sooner or later, caught up in the process of extermination as anonymous laborers. With her story, Alexandra had led us to one of the lesser known elements of the Holocaust by bullets: the handling of the goods stolen from the Jews. "I stole buttons from a Jew's clothes—four of them!" Throughout her testimony, she continually repeated: "I was often afraid that the Germans would find out and execute me!"

One pressed, the other sewed. Girls used as forced labor and associated with murder.

The cook, Hanna Senikova, 74, Romanivka, Nikolaïev region,
July 28, 2006

A ghost town of sorts, the village of Romanivka looked abandoned. Most of the houses were in ruins, overrun by wild and invasive vegetation. The abandoned houses had no roofs, doors, or windows, doubtlessly taken for their metal. A man, burdened with tin milk churns, pointed out to us, before he disappeared, a path covered with grass: "Down there, on the right, lives Hanna." She was, he told us, very old. The village, lost under the luxurious vegetation, reminded me of the hamlets of Burkina Faso. The heat was stifling.

I caught sight of Hanna in the distance, frail and dignified, very upright, sitting on a tree-trunk in the shade. Suntanned, with light blue eyes, she greeted us warmly. She immediately agreed to talk. In a few minutes I was sitting beside her, ready to listen to what she barely dared recount.

Hanna told us that her aunt had been requisitioned as a cook by the Germans. The Nazis had wanted a banquet to be set up for them, during the execution of the Jews. She herself saw the Jews' clothes being sorted. She was nine at the time these events took place. In her testimony, the description of a buffet washed down with plenty of alcohol was mixed in with the account of the death of Jews who awaited their execution in the schoolyard. At the end of the meal, there had been a thousand Jews fewer. A few days after, no trace of the Jewish community had been left in town, it had been struck off the human map.

Patrick Desbois: Were there Jews in the village before the war?

Hanna Senikova: Yes. This village was called the "Jewish Colony." It was called Romanivka only after the war. Before the war, it was a very large colony with more than a thousand houses.

P.D.: Was there a kolkhoze?

H.S.: Yes, there were two, because it was a very big village. The first kolkhoze was called the "Third International" and the second "Tarioupa." One was on this side, the other on the other side, behind me. The old-timers remember these two kolkhozes.

P.D.: What did the kolkhoze produce?

H.S.: It kept cattle but the main activity was the cultivation of wheat. There were several farms but not as many as after the war.

P.D.: What happened when the Germans arrived?

H.S.: We were children. Our mother had taken us to the cellars to hide us because we were afraid of the Germans and we had just been told that they were already behind the hill. The Jews stayed in their houses. The Germans arrived on motorbikes. I don't remember how many there were. They had ammunition belts on their chests. I remember that the walls of the houses in the village were made of stone. The Germans took some of these stones and threw them against the Jews' houses, laughing. On the walls of the village council were images of Stalin, Lenin, and Hitler, with fire coming out of his mouth. The Germans shot at the picture of Stalin but not Lenin.

P.D.: Did the Germans capture the Jews straight away?

H.S.: They didn't touch them that day. The Jews didn't come out of their houses. Then the Germans came back about a week later. They told them that they were going to take them to Israel and that three trucks were coming to pick them up. All the Jews' possessions were requisitioned—cows, pigs . . . I remember that the

Germans requisitioned my aunt to cook for them. They wanted to eat nothing but large pieces of meat; they didn't like small ones. Then some of them shot the Jews while others ate and drank. Then, those who had eaten went to shoot the Jews again while those who had been shooting them before came to eat. They killed them in groups of 25 people. The mothers were carrying tiny children in their arms.

P.D.: When the Germans killed the Jews, did they take them all together to the pit or in groups?

H.S.: In groups of 25. They made them undress completely, young and old alike. They even made the women take down their hair, in case they were hiding jewels in them.

P.D.: Did they shoot people at the edge of a pit? Had a pit been dug?

H.S.: They shot them next to the school. They had first forced them to dig two pits, as big as silos. But they only used one. The second one stayed empty to put the Russians in. They thought they would shoot Russians there but in the end they didn't.

P.D.: How long did the shootings last?

H.S.: I don't remember very well. I know they began shooting in the morning but I don't know when they finished. I don't know what time their orgy finished. They were drinking, singing. They were drunk. They were shooting at the same time. One could see little arms and legs coming out of the edge of the pit. There was a woman who was very fat; they shot her several times but she didn't fall into the pit. They had to go up to her and push her in.

P.D.: Did the Germans ask to be served food near the pit?

H.S.: Son, the Germans didn't ask! They took the animals from the Jews by force and they made Russian cooks prepare food for them.

These women are no longer alive. My aunt was among them. She is dead now. They threatened them with a machine gun. They had made a fire and turned houses upside down, taking pots. They had vodka in their trucks.

P.D.: Do you remember what the Germans wanted to eat that day?

H.S.: They would certainly have said what they wanted in advance. The *staroste*[2] and the police would have given the order to slaughter animals and prepare them. There were 25 Germans with us. They arrived in three trucks. They sat down behind the truck on the edge of the pit. They had schnapps and other items in their trucks. My aunt told me not to go far from the house as I looked like a little Jewish girl; I was very thin with curly black hair.

P.D.: How many Jews were shot at the same time?

H.S.: Two soldiers shot at 25 people with a machine gun. The others were sitting down and eating.

P.D.: Was there an officer who called the soldiers whose turn it was to shoot?

H.S.: There must have been, but I don't remember, I was small. I know that some of them had stripes on their shoulders. I remember that my big brother had a friend who was with him in class, in sixth grade. They often played together in the garden. When the Germans arrived they killed all the children except this boy. Then he went to the Germans and said to them: "Now that you have killed all my family, kill me." The Germans burst out laughing. The boy, frightened, went to my aunt. He had told them that his mother was Polish. The Germans had said to him: "If it's true, prove it: show us her papers." The boy managed to find his mother's papers among the clothes of the thousands of people who had been shot. The

Germans then told him to go where he wanted, that they wouldn't shoot him. My aunt took him in because she didn't have any children. When she died, he came to live with us. Then he left for Stri where he was killed by the Banderistes.

P.D.: Who guarded the Jews during the shootings? The Germans, the police?

H.S.: The Germans and the police, including Kotyha Gricha, a man from the town of Kaluga . . . But they all died in prison and are no longer alive. They were sentenced to 25 years in prison. It was mainly the Germans who guarded the Jews.

P.D.: Did they kill the men and women together?

H.S.: Yes, they counted 25 people and took them to the edge of the pit. Those who could not walk were carried by their parents. The children who were in strollers were carried in their parents' arms. They were also naked. When the Russians were requisitioned to fill in the pit, there were tiny arms and feet poking out of the surface.

P.D.: How did they shoot the children who were in their mothers' arms?

H.S.: They made the mothers carry their children below the chest so that they could get the mother in the chest as well as the child.

P.D.: Did people fall into the pit wounded, not dead?

H.S.: Yes. I don't know if it's true but I was told that a Jewish man who spoke Russian very well, without an accent—the Jews often pronounced 'a' in a very strong way, but he didn't—jumped into the pit without being wounded. He waited until the end of the shooting to get out. The Germans never went near the pit. They appointed Kothya to guard the pit. The man asked Kothya to let him come out of the pit but he killed him instead.

P.D.: Did every German have his own weapon?

H.S.: Each one had his own weapon and they hung them on iron nails in the trees. The Russians said that if they took these weapons, they could kill the 25 Germans. Especially as these weapons were not far from the Jews but the Jews never touched them. They did what they were told.

P.D.: **Were these Germans young?**

H.S.: They were young; none of them was over 40. They were called "SS."

P.D.: **What did they do after the executions?**

H.S.: They left immediately, after having eaten and drunk well. They left policemen to guard the pit and to deal with the clothes and the papers that were in the school.

P.D.: **What did the police do with the clothes?**

H.S.: They took what they wanted. They took all the Jews' horses, carts and clothes. The following day, they sold all the clothes at a sort of market. They sold clothes, furniture, chairs . . .

P.D.: **Were these things sold for a lot of money?**

H.S.: I don't remember any more. My mother was in the hospital and she said to us: "Children, don't take any of those things—they are full of blood. I may be poor but I don't want blood in my house." We didn't go. We were only children in the house; my father was at the front. They were three very difficult days, you know. The cattle roamed free in the village, coming and going, the cows mooing because they were swollen with milk. The seven Russian families of the village were afraid that they would be shot in the remaining pit. My mother had told us not to go out. And that if we had to die that we should go and get her with a wheelbarrow so that she could die with us.

P.D.: **Did they also take the animals that were left in the Jews' houses?**

H.S.: It wasn't the Germans that came to take them, it was the Russians. They came to take them, kill them and sell them.

P.D.: **Did they also sell the tableware?**

H.S.: Yes. They only took the good things—the bad ones were left in the houses. The gypsies came to occupy these houses and then the Germans sent other people to live in them. These people were then sent to Germany and the village was left empty.

P.D.: **Were the Germans who came to occupy these houses civilians?**

H.S.: No, they weren't Germans; they were civilians from other villages, from Zagradovka and Ternokva.

P.D.: **Were people still alive when the pit was covered up?**

H.S.: Who knows?! No one was allowed to approach the pit. Perhaps someone was only wounded and it took the whole night for him to die—we can't know . . . The morning after the execution, we had to go and get the young boys from other villages to fill in the pit with their spades. There were no young people in our village.

P.D.: **Is there something you would like to add that we haven't asked you?**

H.S.: I don't know. No one has ever asked me such questions in my life. Thank you for what you are doing and excuse me for not remembering everything. I have told you everything I remember. I have invented nothing.

In Ukraine there were no extermination camps, no barbed wire to separate the condemned from their assassins. The former suffered in agony while the latter asked the waitress for more meat, sitting around a large dining table.

I had already heard a similar story in Rawa-Ruska. The Germans had grilled chickens less than 10 meters away from the gaping mass grave "which screamed." Witnesses also said that the gunmen sucked mints while they shot.

The point of view of the outsider, of the "requisitioned" that I met, took in both the assassinated and the assassins in a single gaze. I remember that during a study seminar on the Shoah at Yad Vashem, the teachers repeated that, very often, the history of the Shoah was written from the point of view of the victims or from that of the assassins, and that it was practically impossible to write it integrating the two points of view. The point of view of the outsider allows us to understand the Shoah by integrating both victim and oppressor. It is an untenable point of view. It is difficult to hear that a German gunman asked for cold meat and vodka because he was hungry and thirsty, and that he placed his pistols on the table while naked Jews were to be murdered less than 10 meters away from him. It is difficult to hear about the everyday life of the assassins of the Reich while their victims, without barbed wire or camp, waited for death, weeping, with all their family. Yet that was the Shoah. Human beings who killed other human beings, believing they were superior beings killing sub-humans.

―――――――――

Jews were brought from all the villages in the district and locked up in the German police station. Early in the morning they were shot, naked, behind the police station. Those requisitioned for this execution were numerous. Among them, the Germans requisitioned two horse-drawn carts with their owners to transport the Jews.

The police station also forced several young boys of around 16 to guard the Jews at night. If a Jew escaped, the requisitioned guards would be shot. I dared to ask the forbidden question: "Were there Jews who tried to escape?" Ivan Lichnitski, the witness who told me the story of this assassination, replied: "Yes, two Jews tried to escape and my brother had to kill them."

The discomfort was palpable. In this case, the border between requisitioned and guilty was very thin.

I also remember a requisitioned woman we interviewed in Kalininskoye, Crimea. Maria Kirielenko stood outside her grey metal door in the cold. In the back yard of her house I had caught a glimpse of her two sons, scrap iron merchants, perched on a large truck made of dark red metal. Throughout the interview they had been throwing large pieces of iron into a dump-truck, with an occasional questioning look at their mother, who was talking about the assassination of the village Jews to a priest.

With a hard expression, Maria recalled the violence with which the doors of the houses were smashed to take out the unfortunate Jews and push them toward the place of their execution. Maria explained to us how she was requisitioned to fill in the mass grave with her spade. Before I heard her testimony, I had thought that the Germans mainly requisitioned men for this kind of hard labor. It was not the case. Maria described the clothes of the Jews blowing about in the wind in the schoolyard where they had been forced to undress before running toward the pit.

Most of the people who were requisitioned were assigned to filling in the pits. It wasn't just a case of filling in lifeless ditches, as the shot

Jews were very often only wounded, not dead. Everywhere, from east to west, north to south, the witnesses always ended their testimonies by muttering: "The pit moved for three days."

The list of the minor trades involved in the extermination is long and on each trip it got longer. There were those who mixed lime with the blood of the Jews; those who tied the Jews' clothes up in bundles and then loaded them onto carts; those who patched up the clothes; those who prepared food for the oppressors during the executions; those who drove carts full of hemp or sunflowers with which to burn the bodies; those who placed sunflower or hemp on the layers of bodies; those who tore out the Jews' gold teeth while they awaited their execution, collecting them in a canvas bag that they gave to the Germans in the evening; those who transported Jews in their carts from the villages to the pits; those who stored the spades in their house at night, between shootings; those who packed down the bodies of the Jews in the pits and covered them with sand between shootings; those who surrounded the groups of Jews who arrived at the pit until all the families were shot; those who guarded the Jews to prevent them from escaping; and those who brought ash to clean up the ground after the executions. Most of them were children.

Some received compensation for their work; the Germans kept the good clothes and gave the rest to the peasants. A witness once said to me: "One day we woke up in the village and we were all wearing Jews' clothes." Another told us that his mother had said to him: "Don't take the Jews' clothes; they are covered in tears."

Some had suffered as a consequence of having been requisitioned, like the woman in whose house the Germans requisitioned a room to store the spades. The execution had lasted several days; they had deposited the spades at night and collected them again the following morning. She found it difficult to tell us this. Her farm is isolated and just across from it more than 10,000 Jews were shot. It was only when we put the camera down and her testimony was over, that she told us that the Germans had occupied her house. We immediately got out our equipment again and recommenced filming. Every 10 minutes or so, she took a pill for her heart. I sensed how much agony it caused her to give her testimony. An agony mixed with relief. She recounted the incessant shootings and the cremation of the bodies in an open-topped oven constructed by the Germans.

Thanks to these testimonies, we gained insight into the daily mechanics of the killings.

The Nazis had taken away beauty from everything. The most luscious green landscapes became extermination fields, and Ukrainian children became the hired hands of death. The perpetrators of genocide used everything—cliffs, grain silos, beaches, irrigation wells, ditches. Everything that could be closed off was used as a prison. Schools, town halls, synagogues, wine cellars, police stations, shops, the kolkhoze pigsties, chicken houses, and stables, had become, one after the other, the antechambers of death. The landscape, buildings, and children became, in the hands of the assassins, tools to exterminate the people of Abraham, Isaac, and Jacob.

XI

ESTABLISHING A METHODOLOGY

Can one—should one—talk about a "method" in regard to such a research process as ours? Why were we tramping along muddy paths to gather the testimonies of hundreds of Ukrainians who, as children, had witnessed the assassination of their Jewish neighbors, perpetrated by youths from Germany who were told they were saving humanity?

At the beginning of my research, I thought I would explore at most a hundred villages in the region of Lviv in Galicia, where my grandfather was interned during the war. No more than that. My understanding of the extent of the massacres grew gradually.

In my journal for August 6, 2004, I wrote naively: "I need at most two more trips to finish my research into the mass graves of Ukraine, one to the south, in the Carpathians, the other to the north." The methods that we used then were simple, even rudimentary. I went to Ukraine in a blue van, accompanied by an interpreter, and a journalist friend, Jean-François Bodin, who took photographs and filmed the witnesses with a small camera. By the end of the process, while the interpreter, the van, and I were still there, everything else had changed, bit by bit. At first I had only thought of fulfilling a duty of memory toward the Jews who had indirectly crossed paths with accompanied Claudius Desbois, my grandfather. A year later I found myself, trembling, presenting my work to several great assemblies, most notably in the United States, in New York, and Washington, D.C.

I remember July 20, 2005. I was presenting my research to the office of the Claims Conference.[1] In New York, in the beautiful Museum of Jewish Heritage situated on the southern tip of Manhattan, the large bay windows looked out over the bay and the Statue of Liberty. On both sides, ships were sailing despite the rough sea. All the members of the audience were important people, the heads of various organizations with worldwide recognition for their work in transmitting the memory of the Shoah. Here I was, a little priest from Bresse talking about two elderly shepherdesses from Sataniv[2] who saw the town's Jewish community walled up by the Germans in the cellars under the central market. I was given 10 minutes to talk. I asked for the lights to be turned off and then projected the faces of those who, in Ukraine, had seen the Shoah. I talked about Olena, Anton, and Dora's last words, and of the little Krymchak[3] girl shot at "Kilometer Eleven,"[4] not far from Simferopol. Images of their tear-filled faces, the mass graves, and the fields followed each other on the screen.

The 10 minutes went by very quickly. The ceiling light went on again and the grey metallic curtains hiding the bay windows slowly lifted. Once again we saw the coming and going of the large boats heading out to the sea for distant destinations in the grey waves of the Atlantic Ocean. I went out onto a terrace to take in the sea air and looked at Ellis Island, where so many immigrants coming to live here first arrived. My thoughts ran to all those who, in Ukraine, dreamed of being able to get to this American coast and who lie buried, in the hundreds of thousands, under fields and bushes. To my grandfather and his poultry, but most of all to the Jewish children of Rawa-Ruska, Rata, Belz, Ougnif, Busk, Lviv, Sataniv, and of all the other villages and towns that I had visited in Ukraine.

Then we had a coffee break. Orange juice, American coffee, and kosher cookies were placed on long wooden tables. Several people that I had seen earlier came to talk to me, business card in hand. All were visibly moved and they said, with that typical New York accent: "Father Desbois, I haven't come to talk to you on behalf of my organization but because my family disappeared in a little village in Ukraine. If you go there, could you tell me what you find? We have been without news since 1941."

Here in New York, far from the neon lights of Broadway, for 60 years men and women have had no news of what happened to their loved ones. Many hoped, at the end of the war, that at least part of their family would have managed to escape to the east, to Kazakhstan, Siberia, no matter where. Too often, this was not the case. The memory of the Shoah is primarily held in trust by those people, who want us to remember the millions of Jewish men, women, and children who were assassinated by the Reich. For no reason at all.

Several days after this meeting, I went to the United States Holocaust Memorial Museum in Washington D.C. where I had been invited to present my work to researchers and specialists of the Shoah. The museum, which is a stone's throw from the White House, is made of red bricks in a black framework. I went to the fifth-floor home of the museum's research center. The elevator is rather oppressive, all covered in metal and lit by a dozen circular lamps. Suzanne Brown-Fleming, of German origin, welcomed me and guided me to a workshop already in progress. Ten researchers were waiting for me. For over two hours, I explained my work to them, aided by a PowerPoint presentation and videos. On a screen, a little film of distant images took us to the forest of Lviv. Before stating my conclusion, the room still plunged in semi-darkness, I wondered about my audience's reactions which, I was sure they would not be slow to express. I also thought of all the witnesses, their stories, and their life in Ukraine. My thoughts went to the young people requisitioned by the Nazis to dig a pit or fill it, and to all the little people I met during my research—all those people who do not exist anywhere, neither in official reports nor in German or Soviet archives. At the very best, they are mentioned with use of the passive form: "The bodies were evacuated," "The pits were dug," "The clothes were taken." But by whom? They were the invisible outsiders. Neither victims of the crime nor guilty of it, just present. They sometimes witnessed a large execution, like the one in Bodganovskoie,[5] in what was then Transnistria. Sometimes they saw a smaller one, like the one of the father whom the local Gestapo shot together with his three small children to put an end to his crying over his assassinated wife, right there at the edge of the hamlet.

I also saw in my mind's eye that poor old lady whose house was requisitioned to be a Gestapo headquarters . . . She sat silently with her daughters on a little bench in front of the house, beside the asphalt road. She seemed to be hiding as best she could, with her big thick blue woolen scarf and large glasses with their light brown plastic frames. One of her daughters, the youngest, took her gently by the shoulder and encouraged her: "Come on, mama, speak!" The old lady nodded her head, not saying a word. "No, no, they're not going to deport you to Siberia; all that's finished!" The woman remained firmly locked in her silence. Svetlana calmly sat down opposite her. And then suddenly, in a voice that could barely be heard, she began her story: "The Gestapo was living with us. They had requisitioned the house. One day I was in the garden, just there, behind the entrance gate, and I saw in the distance a Jewish woman coming on foot with her three small children. She was going from house to house to beg for food. I ran as fast as I could to tell them not to stop at our house. The head of the Gestapo saw me from the window; he opened the door and started running after me. When the Jewish woman was in front of us with her children he shouted out to them in a loud voice: '*Juden?*' The woman nodded yes. Then he got out his pistol and shot them, right there in front of my door."

She started to cry, then got up and led us through her house, showing us the kitchen garden, with an area for potatoes on one side, and for corn on the other. She held out her arm: "You see over there, beside the bridge, that is where they buried all the Jews who were shot here." These faces, stories, and words never leave me—wherever I am.

Thanks to this workshop and the opportunity it gave me to connect with all the researchers of the museum's Center for Advanced Holocaust Studies, I realized the impact of my discoveries on the history of the Holocaust. One after the other, the researches described academically what I was discovering on the ground. These meetings helped me understand in full the relevance of my work. It became obvious that my research could no longer be reduced to an empirical approach, however positive. I had to "professionalize" it.

What surprised me most was that the professional researchers who focused on the Holocaust in the Ukraine, and who had been working for a long time in the archives in Washington, immediately recognized the contribution that my research would make in the academic arena. For example, Martin Dean, who had edited a book on Ukrainian collaboration and who was now the editor of an encyclopedia of the ghettoes throughout Ukraine, immediately opened his doors to me. After every discovery I made, we exchanged perspectives, he on the ghettoes and I on the executions. Paul Shapiro[6] told me repeatedly how revealing it was to compare my research on the ground with the microfilm documentation the Museum had been collecting since 1991.

While I kept these contacts going, I went to Munich to present my work again. Édouard Husson,[7] a French German-speaking researcher, had set up this meeting with German researchers. I was quite worried about how they might react to the discoveries of a French priest who was combing the Ukrainian countryside. They listened to me attentively, particularly Dieter Pohl, famous for his research on the Holocaust in Eastern Europe. He came to see me at the end of my presentation and said: "Father Desbois, I had never heard anything about the witnesses you found, especially the requisitioned; they are not mentioned in any German archive." For me his appreciation was proof that I was on the right track. This encounter marked the beginning of an ongoing cooperation with the German archivists and researchers as well.

Several years after the beginning of my research, the president of Yad Vashem, Mr. Shalev, asked me to present my work to an assembly of researchers at the Jerusalem center.

I walked into a packed room and started talking right away, again introducing the faces of Olena, Maria, and Adolf—those humble Ukrainian people whose words had found a way to reach Jerusalem. I was a little worried, for it was not to be taken for granted that a French priest would be automatically accepted in this setting. But it didn't matter; people came to tell me the importance of my work and how innovative it was. The institute itself was trying to identify all the locations where the Jews had been assassinated. I, of course, agreed to share my work with the Yad Vashem museum, and the Holocaust Memorials in Paris, Washington, and Rome, to be used both by researchers and by individual descendants of the victims, so that they could learn where their grandparents were assassinated.

I didn't think on my own of establishing a process or a protocol for my work. It was the number of discoveries and the sheer size of the research that made it necessary for me to envision a structure for my approach. When interviewing Ukrainian peasants, I would accompany them step by step through their painful memories, their memories as children or adolescents. But I had to be cautious and not allow myself to be carried away by their memories and lose focus.

Thorough and comprehensive archival research was vital for my work. One cannot simply saunter nonchalantly into a Ukrainian farm without having first carried out solid historical research. It is a *conditio sine qua non* for a successful interview with a witness, as it allows one to ask the right questions and to decipher the answers.

For years, Andrej Umansky, a small archive genius with an acute intuition, has studied the archives of the German courts that form the basis for legal rulings. He went to Ludwigsburg, near Stuttgart, where the historical depositions and rulings of the German courts are kept. The information they provide can never be complete but nonetheless it allowed us to find out the dates of the big executions, the identities of the units in the villages—police, SS, *Feldgendarmerie*[8]—or indeed references to the pogroms. When I met with witnesses, I already had a framework in place, detailing the circumstances of the killings. During the interview, I would therefore gently confront the witnesses with the information culled from the archives, using very frank questions.

Before going to meet witnesses, we asked ourselves about the topography of the place. Before each trip, Andrej studied and reported on the narratives of German policemen or SS officers who explained how they had watched or participated in the shootings of Jews in a specific village or town in the Ukraine.

He also went regularly to the Holocaust Museum in Washington to work with the museum's scholars and study the Soviet archives. For example, when we had to go to Kovel, in the region of Loutsk, we already knew that some of the assassinations had been committed by a police battalion, the *Ordnungspolizei*,[9] battalion 314. Most of the police in that battalion were of German origin.

Bit by bit we began to understand the organization of the assassins, and how they worked, by performing preliminary research and interrogations. We discovered that before each assassination, a *Vorkommando*, a commando of Germans charged with the logistics but also with the upkeep of the place, arrived in the village to find out the information they needed. Where were the railways, roads, or paths? Was the surrounding land flat? Was the ground made of clay or sand? Were there any anti-tank ditches in the area, or any ditch of some kind? Were there forests surrounding or at least close to the village?

We found ourselves asking the same questions when we arrived in a region. We also had to know the dates of the occupation and liberation of the region, and its status during the occupation. There were several jurisdictions in Ukraine during World War II.[10] The Holocaust took very different forms according to whether one was in the General Government, the *Reichskommissariat,* Transnistria, or in Crimea. Other questions that had a bearing on our research were: Did the front cross the village? Had the village been bombed or burnt down by the Germans? Was the local administration civil or military? It was also important to know what German units were based in the village or town. Only once we had gathered all this information did we meet with the witnesses.

Beyond this solid preparatory work, there was a protocol to be implemented on the ground. We were presented with different situations and decisions: determining whether or not to enter a house, never intruding further than where people wanted us to go. I remember a sailor in Kertch, a town in Crimea that faces the Azov sea and the Russian continent. We happened to run into him in the street and we asked him if he had seen Jews during World War II. He replied with a categorical "no" and went on his way. At the threshold of his front door, he stopped suddenly and turned back toward us, his eyes filled with tears: "The sea was black." The Jews who had come here had all thrown themselves into the sea at Azov to try to achieve their last hope of survival—reaching the Russian shores. Many of them drowned.

When a witness invited us into his or her home, we would take off our shoes in the entrance hall. In many houses, the floor is covered with small rugs placed end to end—lots of little colored rugs, like a worn mosaic. Our shoes would remain there in the entrance, lined up with those of the inhabitants of the house.

At the beginning of an interview, I would try to understand, evoke, and recreate the atmosphere of the time, of the individual's family life. I asked the witness's age, where he or she lived, and their parents' profession during the war. Very often they were farmers in a *kolkoze*. Sometimes the father played the violin or delivered goods for Jewish shops. "Who lived in the village?" This is a key question. All the rivalries and quarrels within the population were used and abused by the Germans to support their murderous intentions. The witnesses might be of German, Polish, or Ukrainian origin, or belong to the Tartar or Romany minorities. I asked if there was a Jewish school in the village and where their school was. They would tell me their childhood and school memories, their family environment and their communal life with the Jews. I asked them to talk to me about the Germans in the village during the occupation. Where did they come from, by what road? What vehicles did they use? What was the color of their uniform? Was there bombing? Was the village burnt down? Step by step I would get closer to the question of the assassination. What happened to the Jews? What was the ghetto like, open or closed? Did they wear yellow stars, yellow circles, or armbands? I would focus my attention on what the witnesses heard and saw. Did people tell them what had happened? Were they requisitioned by the Germans? Where did their information come from? I made note of what their father or mother had told them or what they had said to each other during the shootings. During an interview, making the witnesses aware that we already knew what happened allowed them to speak more freely. They were less afraid of shocking us.

Throughout the interview, I usually stuck to a very concrete account of the events, referring to everyday life at the time. I had to be careful in how I sparked their memories. Objects usually triggered a witness's memory. Numerous elements of the story, which I am already familiar with, unleashed recollections, and functioned as "memory filters": people in the village, horses, carts, poultry, harvests, as well as the cultivating seasons—the cold, the snow, the rain, and the sun—meals, the trees that they climbed on, spades, the house, the stable, children's hiding places, colors, odors, clothes . . . For example, when the Germans asked them to come and bring their spades, I asked them: "What was the spade like? Were you asked to come with your cart? Was there one horse or two horses? What color was the horse?" I know that country people, even 60 years later, remember the color of their horse. I asked them: "When the horses smelled blood, what was their reaction?" They answered that it was hard, that the horses were frightened, and they described the scene to me, often bringing in new elements.

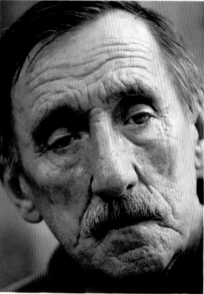

(Above) Lisinitchi (Lviv region). August 2, 2005. Forest of Lisinitchi. Execution site in a forest near Lviv: 47 mass graves.

(Right) Adolf Wislovski witnessed the whole execution process because his family's farm overlooked the execution site. Afterwards, the men of Kommando 1005 burnt the bodies. Several members of the Kommando attempted to escape. Most of them were shot in the fields. His father was requisitioned to transport the bodies to the fires.

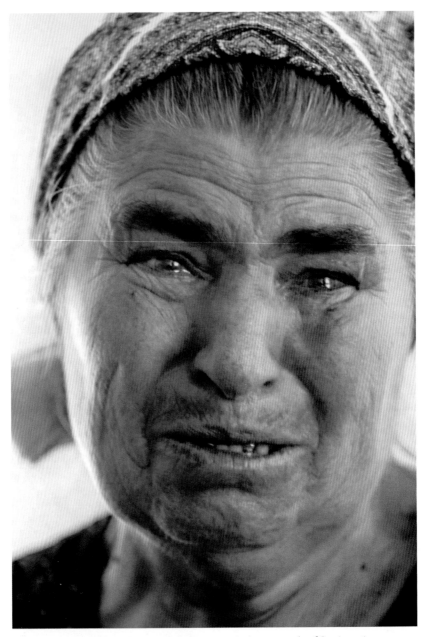

Voskresenskoye (Nikolayev region) July 13, 2006. A commando of Soviet prisoners was used in Operation 1005 to burn the bodies of the shot Jews. When the cremations were finished, the Soviet prisoners were shut into a former chicken house and burned alive. Maria was there: "The flames leapt right up to the sky."

Busk (Lviv region).
August 22, 2006. Eugenia Nazarenko. Her daughter is showing us a photo of Eugenia's father, a violinist requisitioned to dig the graves.

Busk (Lviv region).
(Right) August 22, 2006.
Eugenia Nazarenko would
visit the Havner family to
light their hearth on the
Sabbath. The family was
executed.

(Below) Interview with
Eugenia Nazarenko. Her
father was requisitioned to
dig graves. Her mother hid
with her in the grass, to see
if the Germans were going
to kill him. She told us: "I
couldn't see either the
Germans or the Jews, there
were so many requisitioned
people there!"

Khvativ (Lviv region).
April 15, 2006. With the help of a metal detector, the team of Yahad-In
Unum look for the cartridges that would determine the position of the
gunmen and the site of the grave.

Busk (Lviv region).
August 17, 2006. The archaeologist of the organization Memory evaluates the
cartridges found near the graves. On the base is written their date of manufacture and
an abbreviation indicating their place of production.

Khvativ (Lviv region). April 16, 2006. We discovered a large quantity of
German cartridges.

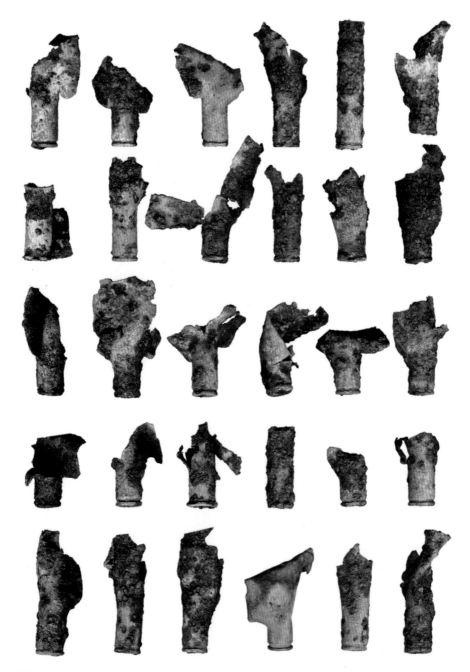

Khvativ (Lviv region).
April 16, 2006. German cartridges found on the site.

On the trail of the Holocaust by bullets.

Busk (Lviv region).
April 16, 2006. Palm Sunday.
Father Desbois interviews a witness
after the Greek Catholic mass.

Lubianka (Nikolayev region).
July 26, 2006. Maria Romantchouk told us that she had seen the cremation of the Jews after the shootings: "It is like bacon. When you grill it, it burns."

Novozlatopol (Zaporojie region). December 30, 2006. The team sits down for a meal in the main village shop. We met witnesses who came to do their shopping there.

Novozlatopol (Zaporojie region). December 30, 2006. From the attic of a house opposite the graves, Ivan Lichnitski saw the carts bringing the Jews of the villages around the Feldengendarmerie. Every morning the Jews came out naked to be shot in three big graves. Requisitioned peasants had to bang saucepans to cover the noise of the executions.

Novozlatopol (Zaporojie region).
December 30, 2006. Marfa Lichnitski told us, in the presence of her husband Ivan, how their Jewish neighbors were loaded onto carts. She could remember their names.

Borove (Lviv region). (Right) March 26, 2007. Yaroslav Galan was grazing his cows near the site of the shootings. He remembered: "While the pits were being dug, the Germans had brought a gramophone to listen to music. One of them played the harmonica. During the shootings, they sucked mint sweets."

(Below) The first mass grave we found. Here the last Jews of Rawa-Ruska were killed, on June 10, 1943. The SS told the Jews to dig the pit and get inside it; they then exploded a mine. "There were bits of bodies everywhere."

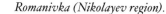

Romanivka (Nikolayev region).
July 28, 2006. The school yard where the Jews were assembled before being taken to the pit. After the execution, their clothes and furniture were sold at an auction in the school over a three day period.

Romanivka (Nikolayev region). Hanna Pavlivna Senikora. Her aunt was requisitioned to cook because the Germans wanted a banquet during the executions. They got up from the table in twos to shoot.

The track along which the victims went to the pit. The school is in the background.

*Torchyn (Volhyn region).
March 30, 2007. Mikhayl
Golovetskyi: "The
Germans requisitioned
80 peasants from the
village, each equipped
with their spade, to dig a
pit 50 meters long, four
meters wide. They told us
to surround the Jews
during the execution. I
refused. They made me
sit on the grass. In the
evening, we filled the pit
in."*

Jovtneve (Nikolayev region).
July 21, 2006. The bodies of thousands of Jews were littered across
the ground of this field. A bulldozer covered them with earth.
Anna Chouprina: "During one of the executions, the inhabitants
of the kolkhoze were requisitioned to dig the graves. Powerless, they watched the

killings. One day my son came home with his back all red. He said to me: 'I refused to
pull out the Jews' teeth, so they beat me.'"

Iltsi (Ivano-Frankivsk region).
August 20, 2005. Part of the Jewish community had been walled up alive by the Germans. Fedor Illiouk was requisitioned to transport the bodies of these Jews on his cart and throw them into the pit. "I had a cart with two horses. I made seven or eight trips from here to Krasnik in the day. Each time I took eight or nine corpses."

"There was a pit of four meters square. They put a plank across it and made the Jews walk onto it in groups of six or seven. The German gunman had asked for a table with smoked sausage and vodka. He shot, then ate, and drank."

I also made sure I respected the witness's point of view and story-telling in order not to influence his or her testimony. I needed to accompany the witness's memory without entering into theoretical concepts or explanations, so as to allow the unfolding of his or her memories of the events, seen through the individual's eyes as a child, unhampered. I had to successfully skirt around the guilt they may have felt about receiving a Jewish garment, about the role they played in the assassination, or even about the simple fact of having been there when it occurred. During the interviews, we were often confronted with horror. I had to accept to hear the unspeakable. I had to get over the disgust provoked by the accounts of infinite sadism. Sometimes we had to stop in the middle of an interview, when the horror had surpassed our understanding. We had to calm ourselves down, catch our breath, drag ourselves out of the narrative, and detach ourselves from the obscenities performed on women and children. Often the witness put himself or herself on the scene only at the end of the testimony. Only at the last moment did he or she tell us that he or she had to take part in it, and what role he or she had played.

We often retraced the witness's steps on the crucial day with him or her, on foot or in the van. I accompanied them, slowly, walking at their pace, asking questions as we went: "What were the Germans' means of transport? How were the Jews brought? In a cart? On foot? Were the Germans violent? Who directed operations?" If a witness told me: "They made people undress," I asked: "And where did they put the clothes? In a box or on the ground? Was it dirty? . . ."

To follow the trail of memory, I physically accompanied the witnesses in their narration. When an old lady told me that she had seen a young Jewish woman place her baby on the sidewalk, I tried to find out precisely where this took place, and only afterwards did I ask her what had happened. She replied that the German soldiers had made an old Jewish lady pick up the baby but because she had been too weak to carry him, they had killed them both. I asked her what they did with the bodies. "They left them on the sidewalk for two days but it became unbearable so then they buried them." I tried to see with the other's eyes to gradually make my way toward the assassinations and uncover the Nazi methodology.

After several days of fruitless research near Lviv, I decided to go to one of the churches in the region. We met a local priest who belonged to an organization that seeks to perpetuate the memory of Ukraine. He proposed to make an appeal during mass to invite people to speak with us. On the way out, three people were waiting for us, including a certain Miron. After exchanging a few words, he said to us simply: "We must go today." We all got into the van and Miron guided the driver to a forest of young trees, the forest of Lisinitchi. We went further and further into the forest, as he explained to us: "I know this forest well. There was a little path that went directly from my house to my school. Every day I saw executions. One day I saw a dead man on the side of the path and I realized it was a Jew who had worked burning the corpses. It was infernal; there was always smoke and it lasted a long time."

I accompanied this elderly gentleman with Svetlana. He found the path and pointed it out to us: "You see, I was there and the body was there." He recreated the scene in his own way. Miron died of cancer a few months after our visit.

He had given us the contact information of an old schoolmate of his. We went to the other side of town to the home of this elderly man who could no longer move. He had been an engineer. In his garden he told us the same story. He saw the executions, saw the trucks full of Jews arriving, and he heard the shootings. "It went on for months."

Down a road, next to a garage, we met another old man, Adolf. Thin, very small, and dark, he described himself as a "militant for memory." He took us to his home, telling us that he kept Polish newspaper articles that talked about the commando charged with the cremation of bodies. He gave us the articles and then said: "I saw the execution of the Italians. I and a friend climbed a tree and we saw the execution of Italian soldiers." We began to understand the extent of this massacre. The testimonies tallied with each other but no one was able to tell us in detail what happened—only that it did happen.

I came across a book written by a survivor, Leon Wells, a Jew who had worked in Yanovska, an extermination camp in Lviv. Book in hand, we retraced the path to the execution site he described and we found ourselves back in the same forest. More proof.

The forest of Lisinitchi was indeed the theater for the massacre of more than 90,000 people.

Andrej Umansky searched the archives of the police and the SS who had worked in Lisinitchi. Even if numerous people acknowledged that they were present at the executions in these records, their assertions remained fairly vague. I went to the Holocaust Memorial Museum in Washington D.C., where massive archives concerning the Holocaust since 1944 have been microfilmed. It is a virtually inexhaustible bank of data that represents 46 million pages that are open to public access, in which one can find also the documents of the extraordinary Soviet commissions of 1944. As soon as the Germans left a place, the Soviets, village after village, opened the ditches, interrogated neighbors, the priest, the mayor, and the survivors, and drew up a document in which they established the facts. They sometimes even drew a sketch indicating the site of the mass graves. But how much could one rely on the Soviet documents, which, although used during the Nuremberg trials, had lost much of their credibility since the revelations about the Katyn affair?[11] Nonetheless, we dissected all the texts of the Soviet commissions. One of them related the order to open all the mass graves at Lisinitchi.

Fifty-seven mass graves were listed. Bodies had been burnt there and the commission indicated that the ashes had been found very deep down in the ground. These statements confirmed the content of the testimonies of Miron and Adolf.

We went back to Lviv to see Adolf and continue the interview. While he was talking to us about the Italians again, he suddenly added: "I also saw Jews. We had climbed the same tree and they were killing Jews." I asked him if he would agree to go with us into the forest. He had not been back there since 1942, although he lived less than a kilometer away. While we were making our way there, Adolf launched into a story:

"Down there is where the trucks arrived, one after the other. First the soldiers with guns went down into the pits, which were at the end of the path, on the left; they were very long, more than 10 meters. The second truck, was full of Jews and went down at full speed. Since some were elderly, they pushed them and as the ground was sloping, some fell down and cried out. Wooden boxes were waiting for them. They got undressed; they had only a few minutes to do it. They lined up in rows and moved forward, accompanied by several guards, until they got to the pit where those who were going to shoot them were waiting."

I asked, "How were they positioned?" He answered, "They were standing around the pit and they were shot with an automatic machine-gun pistol. The first truck left and then another truck arrived." Again I prompted him, "How long did this go on for?" He replied, "Six months. Afterwards they dug up the bodies then they put a fence all around and put dogs and guards there." I asked him, "Where were you living?" He explained, "Where we lived there were no trees. The Germans were afraid of the partisans and so they cut down all the trees. Now there is a forest but at the time of the Germans, there were no more trees, and we lived in a farm high up, so we saw the executions for six months. I remember because some executions took place at night, which woke me up and I and my father went to the window to watch."

I continued, "And the executions of the Italians?" He said, "They were in uniform with their little plumed hats; poor things, they didn't know they were going to be killed so they got undressed peacefully and their clothes were put in the boxes. Since the Germans feared they would escape, there were a lot more Germans but they were led like the others to the pits. Which surprised us because they were very docile. And the houses that you see down there were requisitioned by the Germans to watch over the place. One couldn't go in and the Germans lived in those three houses."

We retraced the steps of the executed with Adolf. We stopped high up, where the trucks stopped. Adolf found it hard to walk and stopped to catch his breath, leaning on a stick that sank into the ground. We went down to the pits where we found a military belt, pieces of straps, metal buttons, and shoe guards on the ground. Instead of a pretty, undulating forest, we began to see the place as the theater of a massacre, a site of extermination. Not just pits where people were killed once, but a place where killings had gone on for six months. Adolf remembered that one day the Germans had asked the Jews to pick up all the pieces of material, shoes, and cartridges so that nothing remained, no trace of the massacres. It was impossible to stop our discussion at that point, and Adolf agreed to speak in front of the camera, which he did for more than two hours. "The last commando of requisitioned Jews who burnt the prisoners attempted to escape by exchanging secret messages in bottles of milk with Polish partisans, and they attacked the Germans from both sides. Some Jews managed to escape but most of them were shot. There were bodies of Jews in all the fields. Peasants were requisitioned to put the bodies on two huge fires that burned permanently." He fell silent, took a break, and then went on: "My father was requisitioned." I was stunned. By this point I had known Adolf for a long time and it was the first time he had told me that his father had played a role in this massacre. "A German came in with a machine gun and told us that we had to come with the cart to transport bodies. There were already bodies all over our garden. We made several trips to bring them all to the fire. We saw everything. Everyone thought my father would be killed at the end, my mother cried, but the Germans let us return home."

Some witnesses needed a lot of time to tell us everything they knew. Often they would start by describing the scene between assassinated and assassins without mentioning themselves, before revealing their role as a witness. Exhausted, my head sank on my shoulders. As I got back into the van with Adolf I asked him: "Did you never come back?" He shook his head and said: "No, for me, this is hell."

A year later I went back to the United States and found, thanks to the Holocaust Memorial Museum of Washington, Wells'[12] contact information. He is the author of one of the first accounts of the Holocaust by bullets. I couldn't get over it: He was living in New Jersey. This book that had guided us for years was for me a history book, an ancient testimony. I had never imagined that the author might still be alive.

I telephoned him. In a hoarse voice he said he was delighted I had called and invited me to his home. I duly turned up in a wealthy suburb— one of those towns uniquely populated by elderly people. Mr. Wells was waiting for us in his house but didn't ask us in; he wanted to eat out. We walked for a long time with this elderly gentleman dressed in American style—jeans, white sneakers, and a baseball cap. We finally got to the restaurant. No customer was under 70. He asked for a quiet table but because there was none vacant, the waitress put us in the middle of the room. Once seated, Wells began in a powerful voice to tell us about the digging up of the bodies and the cremation. Throughout the entire meal I wondered how people at neighboring tables could continue eating.

We finished our conversation at his house: "You see the wall on the left, it is dedicated to my wife's family; they painted. That is why that side of the wall is full of paintings. On the other side the wall is bare because nothing remains of my family."

He told us how he had burnt other Jews with the commando of requisitioned Jews. He told me that the Germans had nicknamed him "Baby." He was 14 years old at the time. I asked him: "What did you do, Baby?" He answered, "I pulled out the gold teeth of the Jews who had been dug up, put them in a bag and gave them to the Germans in the evening. That went on for a long time because there were 90,000 bodies. There was also my friend who was younger than me, who was called the *Tzeler,* the Counter. He was in charge of counting the bodies every evening, and writing the number in a little book."

I asked: "He counted the bodies? What happened to him?" His expression fell. "Of course they killed him." I told him that I knew that they killed the counters. "Yes," he replied, "that is why there is no record of the numbers." I asked: "They made you sleep under some sort of canvas so that you wouldn't see who it was they were killing?" He answered, "Yes, but I was the smallest so I managed to peek under the canvas. I saw all the executions and afterwards we had to go out to undress and burn them. That went on for six months."

I already had many elements as proof: the rather sparse German archives, the archives of the Soviet commission which had opened all the graves, three direct witnesses—a witness who had seen the executions, the member of a requisitioned family, and a Jewish survivor who had "worked" on the site. From tallying these proofs, I could establish the place of assassination. I knew that we had just identified one of the largest extermination sites in Ukraine. Ninety thousand people executed, the majority Jewish, but also Soviet and Italian prisoners . . .

Today the town of Lviv is so developed that the forest of Lisinitchi is an integral part of the town. It has become a public garden. Not a single sign or stone indicates that thousands of people were assassinated there.

Adolf Wislovski, Lisinitchi, Lviv, August 2005

Patrick Desbois: Where were you when you saw the extermination?

Adolf Wislovski: I was high up in some oak trees, down there. I was with two friends.

P.D.: Do you remember where the trucks arrived?

A.W.: They stopped over there, further up. We saw one truck arrive first, then lots of others arrived at the same time. In the trucks there were people, civilians, and then afterwards the soldiers arrived in their cars.

P.D.: Were the civilians Ukrainians, Jews, Polish?

A.W.: Who knows who they were . . . There were different nationalities. In the beginning, in 1941, there were only Jews.

P.D.: What happened then?

A.W.: The trucks stopped. They violently forced the people to get out. The guards surrounded them. There were four SS, in the four corners of the civilian trucks. They were made to undress completely and they were taken down. The people were shouting and screaming but the SS shouted as well "*Schnell*" [fast]. They were guided by the guards toward the pits. They were told to run but of course they didn't have much strength left. It was horrible.

P.D.: **How many pits were there?**

A.W.: We counted 59.

P.D.: **When did they dig the pits?**

A.W.: One or two days before.

P.D.: **Once they had dug a pit, did they kill people and so on?**

A.W.: Yes. When we saw them digging a pit, we knew that there would be a German action.

P.D.: **Did the executions take place in the morning or the evening?**

A.W.: There were some in the morning and in the evening.

P.D.: **Did they kill people in groups or all at the same time?**

A.W.: They killed all the people in the truck at the same time.

P.D.: **Did another truck arrive immediately afterwards or was there a long time between the trucks?**

A.W.: It wasn't regular. There could be two in one day, there could be a day or two without executions.

P.D.: **After killing people, did they put soil on top of the pit?**

A.W.: They immediately put soil. The place was left open and in the first few days and months after these first actions, one could come and look; later, it was no longer possible and no one could come. The Germans were continually stopping their vehicles, waiting for people to be brought to them to be shot. They were everywhere in the fields and on the roads.

P.D.: In your opinion, how many farms were close enough so people could see the executions from their windows?

A.W.: The farms up there could see—there were two or three.

P.D.: Did they think that they were going to be killed since they could see everything?

A.W.: They heard the shots and the cries; they understood what was happening.

P.D.: Who was in these teams of gunmen? SS, Gestapo, non-Germans?

A.W.: SS and Gestapo. We could tell by the signs on their collar. There were Russians and perhaps others, locals. They were digging the pits. The Russians still wore their uniforms. The Germans were more numerous.

P.D.: How many massacres of Jews were you able to see?

A.W.: I only saw one and it was atrocious. But I heard the other shootings and the cries.

P.D.: What were your reactions when you heard the shootings? Did you go and watch at the window or did you not want to?

A.W.: The first time, I went to look because it was the first time I had heard all that.

P.D.: How did you know later that the Italians were also going to be killed?

A.W.: They had already been massacred here; I came here the first time to see the Italians.

P.D.: Did they also make them get undressed?

A.W.: A bit further down, they got undressed.

P.D.: Were they accompanied by soldiers, as with the Jews?

A.W.: Yes. Even more soldiers surrounded them. There were really a lot of people who were shot here. So there were lights and sentries; they also shot at night—they had put in electricity.

P.D.: Was there a fence, barbed wire?

A.W.: Yes, they put them up later.

P.D.: What year do you think they shot the Italians?

A.W.: 1943, 1944. In winter 1944, I would say.

P.D.: Did the Italians cry and shout? Did they know they were going to be killed?

A.W.: No, I didn't hear them crying. Perhaps they didn't understand.

P.D.: When you saw the Italians being killed, were there cremations yet?

A.W.: No, not yet. In spring 1944 we saw the smoke rising and it was hard to breathe. We didn't understand what was happening. Then, at night, we saw that they were throwing something in the fire. We saw everything: there was light, towers, barbed wire.

P.D.: Did people go out to look?

A.W.: We saw enough from the window; perhaps some people watched from their doorway.

P.D.: When these fires were finished, what do you think happened?

A.W.: After, the prisoners went in the direction of the pits and attacked the guards during the night. They tried to transmit messages to the Polish partisans when they were planning something. With their help, they attacked the Germans on both sides. It was terrible; we heard the shots and everything was illuminated by the light of the rockets. Later on we knew what had happened but at first we were frightened. We heard the shots and cries. A lot of people were killed. In the morning, we could see the bodies.

P.D.: Were the Jews killed just behind your houses?

A.W.: Yes. In the fields themselves.

P.D.: All around? That means the Jews managed to get out, that they fought?

A.W.: Yes. There were a lot.

P.D.: What happened to the bodies of the Jews who were killed in the fields?

A.W.: They requisitioned people to bring all the bodies here.

P.D.: Did you take part in that?

A.W.: My father, yes.

P.D.: How were people requisitioned? Did Russian or Ukrainian soldiers go and take people from their houses?

A.W.: They received an order. The Gestapo came, saying: "Do you have a horse?" to transport the bodies.

P.D.: Did the Gestapo speak Ukrainian?

A.W.: Yes and Polish too. Some of them spoke Polish. They only had two words to say, so what was the point of interpreters?

P.D.: Did the Germans burn the bodies of the Jews?

A.W.: Yes, it took several days. It was clear to us that it would be our turn next and that they were going to put us in these pits.

XII

YOUR BROTHER'S BLOOD

Since childhood, I have been aware that God and evil exist. My first theology assignment at the seminary was entitled "The Providence of God, the Existence of Evil." I believe I have yet to finish the assignment . . . I have always believed in the Providence of God, accomplishing people's destinies. And, at the same time, I have always been aware of the abominable face of the world and the abominable skill that a man can employ to kill another man. I received this belief and this vision of society from my family and my Church, but also from the Jewish tradition. A single human race, created in the image of God. Each person is unique. In my eyes, they didn't kill Jews, they killed Ossik, Tania, Anna . . . The assassins spoke about saboteurs, Bolsheviks, Jews, or gypsies. Sometimes they related, laconically, certain details about their mass crimes. Of course, since they never forgot to record statistical data which was of considerable importance for the Reich, they reported the number of people they assassinated. For me, as a priest and a man, in village after village, interview after interview, I worked to recover the graves of Anna, David, and Anton.

The time I spent in Ukraine was not just an opportunity to do research, but was also the occasion for meetings with unforgettable human beings. After all these years, the people I remember most are those who had a friend who was assassinated. Olena, who spoke about a friend of her mother's; another who saw her childhood friend taken into the fields and shot by a *Volksdeutscher*[1] who then brought a cart of sunflowers to burn her friend and all the Jews who had been killed in the preceding weeks. I also remember the people who conveyed the last words of the dead. Like Anna, whose Jewish friend, knowing that she was hidden in a wood shack nearby, turned toward her when she was about to be shot and said: "Farewell, life." Or that Ukrainian who saw her Jewish friends being taken away in a cart. Seeing her crying, one of them got down, took her in her arms and said: "Don't cry, we are going to Palestine." She told me: "I knew very well they weren't going to Palestine because very early that morning I had gone to look after my cows and I saw the pit that had been dug at the edge of the village." These people who, until this day, have kept the memory of their friends' last words.

I also met many local priests who helped me enormously with their parishes. Like the Greek Catholic cardinal of Lviv, Cardinal Housard, who immediately agreed to a meeting. Entering the large Episcopal palace dominating the town that was his office and residence, I saw that it was completely empty—not a single piece of furniture or carpet. At the beginning of the interview he asked me, very simply, whether I needed a car. To my great surprise, he added: "Because I have a car with a driver and with him we discovered many mass graves. I remember one of them, it is hidden behind a psychiatric asylum. If you want, my chauffeur will come with you and he can show them to you." I was delighted to have his support; he is a major figure of the Church, and he immediately offered to help me. Our conversation revolved solely around the mutual assistance we could give each other. I later learned that he had been informed of my forthcoming visit by Cardinal Lustiger.

I also remember the Greek Catholic priest in Busk whom I met on Palm Sunday, seven days before Easter. Almost the entire village had come to church, the children were playing outside, and the mass was broadcast through loudspeakers. During the service, he issued an "appeal for witnesses." No sooner had the mass ended than people, in their best clothes, with their beautifully decorated palms, gathered around the church to be interviewed.

I also remember that Polish priest who officiates in the Catholic parish of Berdiansk, in eastern Ukraine, near the Russian border. He didn't hesitate for a single second before he asked us to come in. I explained the reason for our visit. With lightning speed, he immediately seized his telephone and began phoning all his aged parishioners, asking them if they had seen something.

In Ukraine, both Catholic and Orthodox priests were always ready to help us. We arrived without warning and they often invited us to stay for a meal. I never sensed the smallest hint of reticence when I mentioned the shootings of the Jews or the Romanies by the Nazis.

Establishing the truth is also important to our understanding of our region. How can we build a new Europe based on the effaced memory of the victims of genocide, on the forgotten bodies of the victims, without in this way allowing for even greater injustices in the future? No one who is responsible for genocide should ever think it possible to hide their crime. My work is primarily an act of justice toward the dead, with the aim of creating awareness of the barbarity and wrong of what occurred, but also of preventing future genocides. Another purpose of my work is to convey the message that, even if decades go by, someone will eventually uncover and get to the roots of a genocide, whomever the perpetrator may be. The blood of Abel will not cease crying out to the sky, and will continue to resonate in my conscience. As it is written in the book of Genesis:

> The voice of your brother's blood is crying to me from the ground! (Genesis 4.10)

Anna Dychkant, 77, Busk, region of Lviv, April 29, 2004
Anna was frightened. One of the employees from the land register came to get her. She asked him to wait while she put on her Sunday clothes before getting into our van.

Patrick Desbois: Where are we now?
Anna Dychkant: In Chevtchenko Street, in the Jewish cemetery.
P.D.: Was there a Jewish quarter here?
A.D.: Many Jews lived in the center of town, a few in all of the streets; there were Jewish houses at the end of Chevtchenko Street as well, schools, and several shops.
P.D.: Do you remember what happened when the Germans arrived in Busk?
A.D.: The Germans immediately began building a ghetto for the Jews from our village and from the surrounding villages. There were a lot of Jews in Sokal . . . There were Jews in every village. They were

very often merchants. And then the massacres began. They rounded up the Jews who were young and strong and put them to work. Most of them had to dig pits. Then they brought people to be shot while others dug the pits.

P.D.: Do you remember the first action carried out by the Germans?

A.D.: They assembled the Jews in the center of the town where the ghetto was—which was enclosed . . . I wasn't there, but I was told about it. They made them sit down and then they were shot. They took them into the ghetto in a truck. After, they began killing them down there behind that house, I remember. The Germans had very big dogs. The Jews were digging the ditches themselves. At the end, the Germans requisitioned people from the village to dig. People brought their spades. The Jews were at the edge of the pit, the Germans shot them directly in the back and they fell straight into the pit. Then they put lime on top. I remember a young Jew who was holding twins in his arms. A German went up to him, shot at one child, then the other and the third shot was for the father.

P.D.: Did you see this yourself?

A.D.: Yes. I was in the house down there. I was looking through a hole, trying to see what was happening. The Germans were shouting at the children, telling them not to look, and were chasing them away.

P.D.: Did the Jews have to undress?

A.D.: I saw the Germans down there, where the river Solotvena is, shouting to the Jews, "quickly, more quickly" so that they would walk more quickly. People tried to walk as quickly as possible but they kept tripping.

P.D.: How many Germans were there?

A.D.: Four, six. With two black dogs. The Jews were trying to throw their gold and valuables into the river without being noticed. When the Germans saw this, they shouted at them, then made them walk further on, making them go through a gate. Up over there was a shack. They collected the Jews' possessions in the trucks. They made piles. There was a pile of glasses, of pants. Then they took all those objects to the ghetto. I think the Germans kept the finest things. The Germans made us help them sort out all these things. I had a Ukrainian neighbor who had to help them.

P.D.: Did that go on for several days?

A.D.: I don't remember. Until they had destroyed the ghetto. A year perhaps. The young girls—there was one who went to school with me, Silva, who was very beautiful—weren't killed straight away. Silva had to live with the German commander. The other girls waited on the other soldiers. When the girls got pregnant, they were killed, because they couldn't have children with these people. They asked the Sokal police to take these girls, who were really beautiful, to a place 10 kilometers from Busk to kill them because they didn't want to do it themselves. There was half a truck-load of them.

P.D.: How long did the execution here last?

A.D.: The executions began at dawn, around 5 am. It didn't happen every day. They waited for the arrival of the Jews from the other villages.

P.D.: What month was it? Was it the summer?

A.D.: It was summer, it was hot. At the end, when there were no more Jews in the ghetto, the Russians arrived. Then the Germans came back, then the Russians came again. The ghetto had already been reopened. There were still several young Jewish men and women there. One of them, Rotenberg, didn't look like a Jew—he didn't have a beard or side-curls. He escaped to Sokal, then to Poland, and from Poland to England. Some had heard what was happening in

Poland and that was why they didn't circumcise their boys. The girls didn't look Jewish and they didn't say they were Jews; they called themselves "Anna," like me.

P.D.: Over what period of time did the action here take place?

A.D.: There were very many executions. Perhaps 15 or so.

P.D.: Did people know they were going to be killed?

A.D.: Yes, they knew they were being taken to their death. They shouted and stumbled. A boy who was with me at school knew; he shouted "farewell" and signaled to me with his hands. They killed them with a shot in the neck. Afterwards, they gave the villagers lime to cover the bodies, with earth.

P.D.: Why do you think the Germans chose this place?

A.D.: I don't know. Perhaps because it's a cemetery that is not over-looked by buildings.

P.D.: How many shootings did you see?

A.D.: One. Afterwards, I didn't want to come back here with my friends.

P.D.: Did other children also watch the shootings?

A.D.: Yes. But they watched them once and didn't go back a second time. Because they were shooting all their neighbors and school-mates. It was a small village—everyone knew each other. Every-one was afraid because we knew that they were killing, beating, and shooting the Jews. Some people hid Jews. There was a woman who lived alone who hid an entire Jewish family in her cellar, while two Germans also lived with her. The Jews often decided to hide in the forest so as not to endanger the life of the family that was hiding them.

P.D.: Do the inhabitants of Busk know that there are mass graves here?

A.D.: Today, one can count all the people who were born in Busk on the fingers of one hand. There is only me and my sister. The others come from other towns and villages.

P.D.: Would you like there to be a monument to the people who died?

A.D.: There were a lot of tombstones here but they were used to pave the roads. Before, the cemetery was guarded but not any more. A monument would be very expensive, I think.

XIII

A BURIAL PLACE FOR THE DEAD

On October 5, 2006, early in the morning, I set off for London with Marco Gonzalez, the coordinator of Yahad-In-Unum's activities. I did not know that the crossing of the English Channel would be so quick; it is like going through a long tunnel, with no view other than grey cement. I took my first steps at the large Waterloo station, where a black and yellow taxi was waiting for us. We traveled 20 or so miles, to a Jewish Orthodox neighborhood of small brick houses. I rang a doorbell. A young, friendly man welcomed me, and with a simple gesture beckoned me to sit down at a large oval wooden table. Then a dozen officials of the Jewish Diaspora came to join me. We waited. The president's seat was vacant. Several minutes later, the very elderly Rabbi Schlessinger arrived. All his disciples got up.

The Rabbi sat down slowly, silent and serious, and started to study the several handwritten documents in Yiddish on yellow and white paper that had been previously placed on the table. They were Rabbinical Court decisions that came from various Orthodox courts throughout the world regarding the laws and rules applicable to the bodies of Jews killed during the Holocaust. Picking up a yellow paper, Rabbi Schlessinger raised his eyes and explained to me in English that it had been ruled that the Jews assassinated by the Third Reich were *tsadiqim,* "saints," and that the plenitude of eternal life had been granted them. Because of this, their burial places, wherever situated— under a motorway or in a garden—should be left intact so as not to disturb their rest.

I listened attentively, concentrating hard, so as to understand as best I could, the Jewish religious position on the dignity of the victims of the Holocaust, as well as the *halakhiques*[1] consequences that ensue.

He repeated his explanation vigorously, while his disciples silently acquiesced by nodding their heads. Then he fell silent. Everyone turned to look at me, and I understood that I had to speak.

This situation was in a sense unprecedented. I had been called to meet in this *schul,* as a Catholic priest and the representative of Christian religious tradition to examine the sensitive issue of the violation of the burial sites of the Jews killed in the Holocaust together with Orthodox Jewish legal experts, people determined to scrupulously respect the prescriptions emerging from the laws of Judaism. How could we work together in a practical way to ensure that the places where the Jews assassinated during that horrific century had come to rest would finally be respected?

The debate went on for hours. They examined the legal cases one by one and I explained repeatedly how I viewed, from the perspective of my Christian tradition, what they were saying.

I am well aware that it is hardly the most normal thing in the world for a French priest wearing clerical attire to be examining cases in the light of the framework of Jewish law. Suddenly, I had an intuition. I asked Marco to show them photographs of the various images of the mass graves opened by marauders. When they saw the bones of their ancestors scattered in all four corners of fields, strewn about like little more than trash, it was a terrible shock. They didn't know that several pits had been opened by "gold-diggers." They didn't know that the construction of irrigation channels had disemboweled the mass graves.

That evening, we decided to set up a religious and judicial cooperation so that I would know what rites to perform in the light of Jewish tradition when I came across graves that had been disturbed.

It was raining over London as my associate and I set off on our return journey. As we were making our way to Waterloo station, I thought of the incomprehension, contempt, pogroms, and expulsions that had marked the centuries of relationships between Catholics and Jews, preventing the coming together of our two traditions. I also remembered the beautiful faces of the men and women who, whether Jewish or Christian, had made efforts to ensure that such encounters would be positive, after two millennia.

As soon as I got back, I called Cardinal Lustiger to tell him what had happened.

XIV

THE MASS GRAVES

On December 30, 2006 my team and I were traveling towards Novozlatopol, the capital of a Jewish district which had been created in 1929 to encompass several Jewish villages. We were so cold we didn't know how to warm ourselves. The ground was entirely covered with snow and ice, and our vehicle was advancing painfully slowly. Our boots and coats were useless against the sting of the Ukrainian winter, and we were happy to spend a few hours inside our van. I reread our preparatory document. We had been given the name of a high school teacher, Polina Savchenko, who was passionate about the history of the Holocaust.

We arrived at 3 in the afternoon, famished. There is no restaurant in Novozlatopol. We went into the main shop of the village, which is called Gastronom. I lost no time and looked through the shop windows to see what was inside. Herrings, plastic-wrapped bacon, sausages, three yogurts, white and grey bread sat on the varnished wood shelves. Perfect. We ate our meal in the middle of the grocery store while Polina

Savchenko came to tell us to pick her up later at her house. The days are so short in winter that it was already dark when we got to the town. She could not ask us in because she had guests. No matter, she covered up and got into our van where there were 11 of us already. With the door open despite the bitter cold and the snow, she told us everything she knew, and talked about the educational documents she gathered and the presentations she gave to her class. As the hours went by, I asked her if she knew any witnesses to the executions. She replied: "Yes, but come back tomorrow." And we set off in the night, through the town's narrow dirt roads.

The following day, at dawn, she was waiting for us in front of the grocery. She took us to one of the witnesses. Ivan Lichnitski is tall and wrinkled, with a rather yellow complexion. His wife Marfa, huge and almost unable to move, was wearing a large apron made of blue material, and shuffled along with the help of a stool to support her. The moment our eyes met, we understood each other. Without realizing it, my grandfather had taught me the expression of those who saw the Jews being assassinated.

Marfa had lived in Roter Poyer,[1] one of the 15 Jewish villages of the district. As a child, she saw the Jews being brought to the village from other villages, in carts. They had been told to bring food for two or three days because they were going to Palestine. Pits had been dug and guards had been requisitioned in the villages. She remembered that she had said goodbye to them. Marfa and her husband remembered all their childhood friends; she counted them out on her fingers: Fridman, Udliar . . . She counted and recounted the number of Jewish friends whom she had seen leaving, giving us their first and last names.

Ivan lived in the capital of the district and saw the carts arriving, driven by requisitioned peasants. They had set up a relay, bringing cartloads of Jews from each of the villages, one after the other. He told us that they had been taken to a German gendarmerie where they had been left in a cell overnight, after all their goods had been taken from them, including their clothes and gold teeth, and after being beaten. The following morning they had been pushed out of the gendarmerie in groups of five, naked. They had been taken behind the building where three very long mass graves had been dug and shot on the spot. Two among them had been chosen to pick up the bodies and drag them into the ditches. They piled them on top of each other, one after the other.

At the end of his testimony, Ivan told us that he had seen everything, hidden in the attic of a house opposite, where hay was stored. We asked him to take us to the site of the shooting the following day.

As arranged, we gathered again at his house. We spoke again about the assassinations and he took us to the site of the mass grave. He pointed out the gendarmerie office and together we identified the position of the shooters, of the collectors of the bodies, and of the first, second, and third open pits. We numbered the pits, taking photos. He pointed out to us the window from which he said he had seen everything. Guillaume climbed up to the attic and pushed open the wooden flap of the skylight to recreate the scene from the point of view of our witness.

We collected this information and found other witnesses who confirmed the site of the assassinations. Using GPS, we marked down the coordinates of the mass graves, in case the area had been modified by the construction of a house or the installation of irrigation channels . . . Then we carried out a ballistic enquiry. Micha explored the area around the pits and found several cartridges—not many because the field had been thoroughly worked over every year. Micha identified the cartridges and put them in different bags. We also took photos and recorded the GPS position for every cartridge. Thanks to the information gathered from Soviet and German archives, we knew that there had been assassinations; we also knew the approximate number of deaths, but we did not know exactly where, when, and how they had taken place. All this was clarified by Ivan's and his wife's testimony.

When we went back to see Ivan, he told us that his brother had been requisitioned by force to guard the Jews during the night, and that other peasants had been recruited in the morning to bang saucepans to muffle the cries of the Jews. One of the villagers had been requisitioned to play the Ukrainian drum every morning. One day, the drummer had not been able to take it any longer. Seeing a *Feldgendarme* beating Jewish children, he had thrown himself at him. The German had shot him and thrown his body in the pit along with the Jews from the 15 villages.

In this case, we were able to recreate an entire assassination scene.

Marfa and Ivan Lichnitski, Novozlatopol, region of Zapojie,
December 30, 2006, first interview

Patrick Desbois: What did your parents do for a living?

Ivan Lichnitski: My father abandoned us when I was still small. My mother did all kinds of work. She worked as a nurse, and she also made bricks. She mixed straw with other things, and then they built houses with them. The Jews lived in these brick houses before the war—they had money.

Marfa Lichnitski: My parents worked in the kolkhoze. My father was head nurse. We first lived in Poltava then, after the great famine, we went to live in a Jewish village. My mother often said that the Jews had saved us from hunger. They helped us a lot.

P.D.: Do you remember the first time you saw the Germans arrive?

I.L.: Yes. It happened without any fighting. Our soldiers had already left. They arrived and began to occupy our village.

P.D.: Where did they come from?

I.L.: From Guliapol.

M.L.: I remember that when the Germans withdrew, one of our scouts came to tell us that our men had just liberated us. But I don't remember the arrival of the Germans. I remember the occupation and the Germans pillaging the Jews' houses. We hid in a gully. We were frightened; they were shooting the cattle.

P.D.: Mrs. Lichnitski, were there Jews in your village before the war?

M.L.: In Poltava, there weren't any. The village six kilometers away was a Jewish village. Some lived there the whole year and many came there in the summer to visit their grandparents. They came from Zaporojie and from many other towns. Not all these people succeeded in evacuating from there. All those children and young people had to stay in the village, when the pillaging started. With other children, we went to see what was happening. People were shouting, crying, and we cried along with them. They had taken the Lerners, the Birmans and the Shoyhets. I don't remember the other names but there were six families in all. They were old people but also their children—particularly young women with their children. They put them all on carts and took them somewhere. We learnt later where they were taken. That is all I saw with my family.

P.D.: Had the Jews who came from the towns been there for a long time?

M.L.: They came for the summer. They arrived in June and should have left in August but they weren't able to leave. There were children and grandchildren. They stayed here and were killed in Novozlatopol.

P.D.: Were there police in your village?

M.L.: There was only one policeman in our village. The headquarters was here, in Novozlatopol.

I.L.: Everything was here: the police, the gendarmerie, and the *Kommandantur.*[2]

P.D.: Were the majority of the inhabitants of your village Jewish?

M.L.: Of course, and Novozlatopol was the headquarters of the Jewish district, which comprised 15 villages. They don't exist any more today.

P.D.: Who perpetrated the pillaging? Neighbors, the police, the Germans?

M.L.: People came from Novozlatopol to pillage Jewish houses. People were frightened, they ran away.

P.D.: During the pillaging, did they go into the houses and make the families come out? Did they force open the doors?

M.L.: The doors were not closed. They entered and took what they wanted. Later they began taking them away in carts.

P.D.: Could the Jews take their possessions with them?

I.L.: They duped them so that they would take their most precious objects. The Germans took the most valuable objects and gave the rest to the gendarmes and the police.

P.D.: Where did the carts bring them to in Novozlatopol?

I.L.: They brought them here, where the memorial is today. A bit further on there was the gendarmerie. They put the Jews in the cells. They took boys born in 1928, 1924 and 1926, gave them a machine-gun and told them to guard the cells. If one of them managed to escape, the boy was shot. They kept them around two days, the time it took to fill the cells. Then they forced the Jewish men to dig a pit and to build a fence and they shot them all in this place. The pit was very long—it must have been 20 meters. It was surrounded by a fence two meters high made of planks. The fence had a door that led into the gendarmerie. They took the people to the pit through that door, and shot them with a bullet [in]to the back of the neck. In the pit itself there were Jews arranging the bodies all along the pit. Once it was full, they were shot in their turn. They brought all the Jews from all the Jewish villages around here.

P.D.: Were there Jews who refused to go?

I.L.: Of course, but what could they do? The police had truncheons and weapons.

P.D.: Did they take the jewels and other possessions from the Jews in the cells or just before shooting them?

I.L.: Before shooting them. They took gold, silver, the things that were in good condition; suits and the rest, in poor condition, they threw into the street and set fire to it. Then they undressed the people who were wearing underclothes.

P.D.: Were they killed in groups of four or five or in large groups?

I.L: They shot them in groups of five or six. The police and the guards had to bang empty buckets to cover the noise of the shooting. Others led them there, mothers carrying their children in their arms or by hand. They were beasts.

M.L.: It was a genocide. Our Rada[3] has decreed that our people were the victims of a genocide but the Jewish people also suffered a lot. My mother told me that the earth moved for three days. Small children were thrown in alive.

Polina Savchenko: It is said that in a village near Novozlatopol there was a musician. He played the *buben*[4] and he was requisitioned several times to play it during the executions. He couldn't bear it. One day, when he was being taken home, he saw a young girl hiding behind the hospital. He said nothing. He went back in secret and saved her and her son. She later became a primary school teacher. Neighbors helped transport her to Dontsk because she could have been noticed with her son. After the war they met again at the memorial.

P.D.: How many days did these shootings last?

I.L.: They brought them here three times. The shootings lasted two or three hours. The next group to be shot had to fill in the pit and dig another for themselves. The guards would do it when there were no more Jews to do it.

P.D.: Did they stop the traffic on the roads during the executions?

I.L.: No. Everyone hid. With other boys, I climbed up to the attic of the pharmacy and we watched what was happening. When they saw us, they shot at us but they didn't hit us, thank God.

P.D.: Were there Jews who tried to escape?

I.L.: A very beautiful young girl with very long hair jumped over the fence. She managed to run to the shop where she was caught and dragged by her hair back to the pit.

P.D.: Were the village police tried at the end of the war?

I.L.: They all escaped, the *starost* and the police. Two *starost* were hung and the others managed to escape.

Marfa and Ivan Lichnitski, Novozlatopol, region of Zapojie,
December 30, 2006, second interview

Patrick Desbois: What exactly did you see when the Jews were taken?

Marfa Lichnitski: With a friend, I was walking beside the pond when the Germans arrived; our parents were frightened for us. They ran to us, saying: "What are you doing? You will be taken too." So we all went to hide in the house. And that is where it all began. We saw everything. The Tsillernies lived right next door, and in the house behind that lived the Friefelds. People were shouting and crying and they were being loaded into carts. They were told to take some things with them as they were going to spend the night somewhere. Their bundles were also thrown onto these carts and then they were forced to get in. When they had been taken away, we went out. We were crying; we were sorry for our friends. They were 10 or 11 years old. I don't know what happened afterwards because we didn't live close enough to see. The people didn't know that they were being taken to be killed. They had been told to prepare food and take clothes; that meant they were being taken somewhere. They didn't doubt that and neither did we. No one knew. Then, when the rumors began to circulate, we knew that they had been brought here to Novozlatopol.

P.D.: Did you know people who were requisitioned to guard the Jews?

Ivan Lichnitski: My brother was requisitioned. I know that he had to shoot two people. Two armed policemen came in the night and said: "Get up, get dressed and come with us."

P.D.: Was it the same gunman who shot all the Jews or was there a different gunman for each person?

I.L.: There was one gendarme who shot them. Two others brought them, hitting them with sticks. The children were crying.

P.D.: Did they kill people in the morning, mid-day, or in the evening?

I.L.: They began a little before lunch and everything was finished by the evening. According to the rumors, the two first pits contained about 200 people.

P.D.: Did your brother also have to fill in the pits?

I.L.: If he was part of the guard team, he had to do it. Once, the guards stole jewels from a Jew. The Germans said to this Jew: "If you can recognize the guards who took your valuables, they will be shot." The Jew pointed them out and they were shot with the Jews.

P.D.: Were the jewels taken from the Jews before they died?

I.L.: They did it before killing them. They made the Jews undress to their underclothes and took all their things. All this happened in the cells

P.D.: Were all these clothes and objects stored in a special house in the village?

I.L.: Everything was kept in the gendarmerie. Afterwards, perhaps they sent them somewhere in a truck, who knows? They were very beautiful things.

P.D.: Were all the pits filled in at the end of the executions?

I.L.: They filled the pits immediately after every execution. The earth was still moving. They filled the last pit with the last victims, filled it in and everything was finished.

P.D.: For how long did the earth move after an execution?

I.L.: About two days. There were dead people, wounded, and people still alive. Not everyone was killed on the spot. Some were only wounded.

P.D.: How many executions did you see from the roof?

I.L.: I saw the first two pits being filled, not the second.

P.D.: Did you tell your family what you had seen when you went home?

I.L.: Yes. What could they say to me? They felt sorrow for these people.

P.D.: Thank you very much. Do you agree for your testimonies to be put into the archives and museums?

M.L.: People must know the truth. The Rada recognized the genocide of the Ukrainian people during the famine of 1932–1933. But the Jewish people also suffered a lot. If you read a book about Babi Yar, you can't sleep for a week. All I saw was the Jews being arrested and taken away but when one knows how they were shot and thrown into the pits alive . . . It seems that when the spring arrived, people couldn't breathe, the smell was so strong.

I.L.: There was a man in our village who escaped before the Germans arrived in our village. But he was caught elsewhere with all his family. His family was shot but he fell into the pit alive. During the night he managed to get out of the pit. He came back here after Liberation.

M.L.: I remember that he helped us cook. He told us what had happened and that the pit was very full when he fell inside alive. That evening he got out of the pit. He was a cook in the sanatorium. He often told us about that, and that the Ukrainians saved him.

XV

AN EXTERMINATION
IN EVERY VILLAGE

Every witness is unique, a living protest of sorts against the abject annihilation of the memory of his assassinated Jewish neighbors.

On April 6, we were in Bakhiv. We knew that more than 10,000 Jews had been transported here in cattle cars. The train had moved forward until the first compartment had neared the gaping and immense mass grave, dug several days earlier. The doors had opened. Armed guards with dogs had hurried the Jews' descent from the train. The Jews had shouted, cried, and screamed at the sight of the pit that awaited them. They had been surrounded and taken to be killed.

Sixty years later we found ourselves in a revolting place. The soil had been recently turned over. Gaping holes surrounded the memorial. Ridges furrowing the earth exposed long white marks: chalk mixed with blood, thrown into the pit by requisitioned neighbors. Pieces of railway track and nails lay on the ground. A channel had been dug, apparently for water to run along it. All the way along the channel were human bones: femurs and scattered skulls. Indecent and unspeakable. A gold ring, a woman's, was barely covered by sand. She must have thrown it away in desperation, so that the Germans wouldn't get hold of it. I picked it up. My gesture, 60 years later, united me with hers. This ring that escaped the hands of the marauders will become, in museums, the only trace of this unknown woman. We felt nauseous. For the first time, the interpreter went to rest in our blue van. It was too much . . . All was mixed up with a great deal of trash, as always. We found traces of a picnic, a half-empty jar of large gherkins pickled in vinegar. Micha summed it up with a look: "pilfering, pilfering." The site had been ravaged by the hands of those who are still looking for the Jews' gold and who had scattered all over the place, like trash, the bones of children, women, and men who were shot here 60 years ago.

Earlier that morning we had met two witnesses. A woman, Solomia Stolartchouk, pale and tired, had told us that if she spoke about it, she would die. Her hands trembled on her chair. She asked if she would be arrested for having told us what she had seen.

An hour later, we had entered a low, dark house. A girl with a weary and rather helpless air had been chopping yellow spaghetti on a wooden board. I had gone into the room where a man named Timofei Ridzvanouk had been sitting, with his white, cropped hair, and a bucket of trash beside him. Illness and poverty seemed to go hand in hand here. He had searched his memory, his words confused. "I was a shepherd. I couldn't escape the requisition. I filled pits with chalk. They mixed chalk and blood." He talked about the train compartments, the doors that opened, the shouts, the barking, and then the shooting, bang, bang, bang . . . bang, bang. "Then silence. Another compartment door opened."

The images of the assassinations had appeared in all their horror. Under his windows, the Germans had killed at least 10,000 Jews in three days, one by one.

All these narratives were similar and yet they were all so different.

The landscape of Ukraine, village after village, east to west, was transforming itself under my eyes into an ocean of exterminations. Whether in Bahkir in west Ukraine, or in Nikolayev in east Ukraine . . . The horrors of the Holocaust were not necessarily exactly the same from one place to another, but they did unfortunately cover the whole country without exceptions.

Olga Bitiouk, Voskresenskoye, region of Nikolayev, July 13, 2006
Olga had hidden under the roof of a friend's house and together they had watched the trucks coming, going, and departing again, unloading Jews on each trip. The Jews were killed and buried before their eyes in three big pits. Later they were dug up and burnt. It all took place under the eyes of a group of children who were later scolded by their parents for going to watch the executions.

Patrick Desbois: What happened to the Jews in front of your house?

Olga Bitiouk: I was with Maria's parents in the attic. From the attic window we saw everything. There was Maria, me, and sometimes her brother. I don't think there were other children; there weren't many children in the area. I remember it as if it were yesterday. A lot of trucks arrived—three, four, five. They went to the first ravine, then the second, and the third . . . They unloaded the trucks as quickly as possible. The people took off all their clothes and went into the ravine. Then they were shot. It was the prisoners of war, who were imprisoned in what had been a chicken farm, who shot them.

P.D.: **Were the people shot from behind or in the front?**

O.B.: I don't know. We were watching from far away. What I know is that we saw it, and that, along with my father and three uncles dead at the front, it made us grow up very quickly in life.

P.D.: **How did you know that these trucks were arriving?**

O.B.: We heard the noise. Everyone knew where they were going and what they were going to do.

P.D.: **Could you go out of your houses to go and look?**

O.B.: No. After a few days, the Germans chased away the people who lived around the ravines.

P.D.: **Could you hear the shots from the house?**

O.B.: Of course—it wasn't far, not more than a kilometer. We heard cries. We were small and we didn't really understand what was happening.

P.D.: **Who do you think it was who got out of the trucks?**

O.B.: They said it was Jews; perhaps there were also other people. Everyone kept silent and everyone was scared. The Germans shot people who spread rumors.

P.D.: **Were the pits covered over with earth in the evening?**

O.B.: No. When the word got out that the Soviet troops were approaching to liberate us, they continued shooting but very hurriedly. Once they had shot all these people, they began burning them. They poured kerosene or God knows what over them. You could smell human flesh burning. They burnt for about a week, and after that they covered over the pit with spades and a bulldozer. But they didn't do it well enough to hide everything they had done.

P.D.: What did the Germans do with the clothes? Did they organize the sorting of clothes on the spot?

O.B.: According to certain people, they loaded the clothes onto carts and trucks and took them all to the same place in the town before sending them I don't know where.

P.D.: Did all these killings take place at the same time?

O.B.: Trucks came day and night. In my opinion, people would not have waited around. The trucks would arrive, be unloaded and then the people were shot immediately. I am not sure because we didn't look all the time.

P.D.: Did you understand that they were killing children?

O.B.: Of course, how could one not have realized that? In those days, children were wiser than they are now. They understood things as if they were adults.

P.D.: Did the Germans arrive by themselves before the trucks to prepare the site?

O.B.: They had already been in our town for some time. There were armed soldiers and canons in our street.

P.D.: Were policemen with them?

O.B.: I don't know. The *staroste* was present.

P.D.: Did they requisition people to cover the ditch a little at night?

O.B.: I don't know. The military prisoners who shot these people must have done it. These prisoners were shot so that no one would know what they had done.

P.D.: Was there a camp of Russian prisoners nearby?

O.B.: Yes, they were in a large chicken farm beside the river. It was surrounded by barbed wire. It was adults who told us that: the children didn't go there. The Germans did what they wanted with these "hostages."

P.D.: Were the Russian soldiers shot in the same place?

O.B.: Yes. They were forced to shoot the Jews, to burn them. They didn't do it by choice. Afterwards, in turn, they were killed too.

P.D.: Did your mother know you had seen these executions?

O.B.: Yes, people told her but our mother didn't go to watch because it was forbidden. You know, we stayed to watch one or two hours, no more.

P.D.: How many pits were there?

O.B.: There were as many as there were ravines, so . . . three. Some said that they selected people and that the small ones went in one ravine, the big ones in another . . . The people were killed almost immediately after they got out of the trucks.

P.D.: Have you seen these different pits for adults and for children?

O.B.: No, those are things I was told. We saw it all from far away, from the attic. No one went close, people were too scared that their family would be shot. The Germans didn't want people to see them but they were seen all the same.

P.D.: Were there people in the pits who were only wounded?

O.B.: They say that when they filled in the pits with spades and a bulldozer, they heard moaning. People must have still been alive.

P.D.: Were these cries heard at night?

O.B.: At night and in the day. Because people were pushed into the ravines and killed day and night. It was terrible.

P.D.: Did some people manage to escape?

O.B.: It seems that one of the prisoners managed to escape. He began running and the Germans began shooting at him but didn't get him. People say he now lives in the village of Vodapoi.

P.D.: Did the Germans take you to see the pits?

O.B.: No, they finished shooting them, burnt them, and then the Red Army arrived very soon after that, and the Germans left. They left a week before our village was liberated.

P.D.: Were there marauders afterwards?

O.B.: I don't think so. What happened was so sad that no one went to steal things.

P.D.: Do you agree for your testimony to be put in archives and museums?

O.B.: As you like. These are things that one cannot forget.

XVI

OPERATION 1005

In 1942, Himmler set up a plan that appears incredible to our modern eyes. It went by a curious and little-known name, Operation 1005. The operation, which lasted from the summer of 1942 to the end of 1944, involved digging up all the victims of the Reich in Eastern Europe and burning the bodies in large furnaces. Special furnaces were designed that could fit up to two thousand bodies. The purpose was to hide all traces of the executions, particularly those performed by the *Einsatzgruppen*. The code name of the operation, 1005, came from the number that was used for the classification of a letter.

The name of this operation is forever associated with the name of a man, SS Paul Blobel. The same man who had previously been responsible for the execution of the Jews at Babi Yar. He was put in charge of the operation in June 1942, and given the task of making all the bodies of those assassinated by the Reich, principally the Jews, disappear.

He organized commandos and sent them to follow approximately the same route that the *Einsatzgruppen* had taken. Paul Blobel also devised a particular technique to make the burning of the bodies more efficient: he had the bodies layered with wood on metal rails as in a pyre; when it was set on fire the cremation was extremely rapid. The same method was frequently used in the extermination camps afterwards.

Since 2000, when I first visited that great sandy field in Poland that was the Belzec extermination camp, I had been puzzled by a practical question: how could the Germans have destroyed thousands of bodies in the remote countryside of Eastern Europe? In Belzec alone almost 500,000 Jewish people were exterminated in several months. Yet, there had been no crematorium ovens. All the bodies had been buried in large communal graves behind the gas chamber. Only later had the bodies been dug up with excavators and placed on fires. How was this possible when the camp was right in the middle of a small town?

During my research in Ukraine, I came across men and women who saw the smoke of the fires, and who had to leave their houses because the smell was so unbearable.

Although surrounded by absolute secrecy, Operation 1005 was doubtless the best known German operation in the immediate neighborhood of the cremation sites during the genocide of the Jews. The same thing was also taking place in Tomachov and in Belzec. A peasant in Belzec explained to me, while chopping wood with his axe: "The head of the camp had requisitioned my wheat and barley sorting machine. He gave me a ticket, telling me that I would get my machine back later. Several months later, as there were no more trains of Jews arriving, I went to the camp door with his ticket to get my machine. The Germans opened the door and I went into the front room where 10 wheat sorters had been placed. Poor Jews had had to turn the handles of the machines. Instead of wheat, they were ventilating Jews' ashes."

That day, I decided to take back, in a van, three wheat sorters, one of which is exhibited in the Holocaust Memorial in Paris.

When I found out about Operation 1005, I realized that it represented the practical implementation of the Reich's denial of the genocide. All perpetrators of genocide deny their genocide, and the Third Reich did the same.

The Reich set up a large machinery employing a large number of personnel in order to destroy the traces of its assassinations. For the Third Reich, denial was above all a technical issue. The 1005 commandos had the task of identifying the communal graves of the Jews, digging up the bodies, counting them, and then burning them. Operation 1005 was kept secret, the SS communicated with Berlin by means of meteorological codes: the number of clouds indicated the graves opened, and the height of the rain the number of bodies burnt.

There were various reasons for this operation. One was anti-Semitic, and could be summed up by the phrase: "They have no rights, not even to our soil." There was also a strategic reason behind this operation. The Germans had learned that whenever the Soviets arrived in a village, the first thing they would do was open the graves, photograph the bodies, and draw up a document with the help of the inhabitants of the village, the teacher, the priest, and any surviving Jews. They would also proceed with a thorough scientific analysis of the bodies. The Reich destroyed the corpses so that the Soviet commissions could not establish proof of their crimes: the war of the dead.

How could I forget Maria's story? She lived in the village of Voskresenskoye, not far from Nikolayev. I arrived in front of Maria's house with Svetlana. Maria appeared, her plaited hair under a multi-colored scarf, her face covered in tears. Just mentioning what she lived through during the war was unbearable to her. Her husband, dressed in blue overalls, rushed out into the courtyard, shouting: "I'm going to call the Soviets. I am going to call the police—my wife won't talk unless the Soviets agree to it."

I have rarely encountered such violence mixed with such suffering. I explained to him that it was only for history, memory, and the archives. Maria managed to contain her sobs: we set up the camera very quickly and she began talking.

She had seen the execution of the Jews from far away. Later, she had seen the bodies of the victims being dug up. A group of Soviet prisoners had been put in charge of the cremation of the bodies; they slept in a small low building around a hundred meters from her house—a former chicken coop transformed into a prison. They were chained to each other. Every day they had to dig up bodies, count them, and set up large pyres for at least 2,000 people, following the technique developed by Blobel. The bodies were placed on wooden crosspieces, themselves positioned on metal beams. Women's bodies were placed below to feed the fire. Once these infernal furnaces had been extinguished and the last traces of the bodies had been destroyed, the Soviet prisoners had been locked up again in the chicken coop. Following Blobel's orders, the Germans had poured oil on the roof of it and set it on fire. "The flames went right up to the sky," Maria recalled, her eyes wide.

I understood later that the SS responsible for burning the bodies had underestimated their work and had got bogged down in destroying the mass graves of the large towns. The advance of the Red Army had interrupted their plan.

Maria, Voskresenskoye, region of Nikolayev, July 13, 2006
Patrick Desbois: What happened to the Jews in your village?

Maria: I didn't understand straight away what was happening. It was
my father who told me that a lot of trucks were arriving at the
ravines. They arrived full of people, the Germans made them get
out, get almost entirely undressed, and then they shot them.
They were treated like cattle. It didn't happen only once. Sometimes few trucks came and sometimes a lot. They were very
quickly ushered down from the trucks and very soon you heard
shots.

P.D.: **Did the trucks arrive one after the other or all at the same
time?**

M.: Many trucks arrived at the same time. There were a lot of people.
Shortly afterwards the execution began. I was not the only one to
see it all. There were a lot of houses above the ravine. But we didn't
live there for very long. The Germans chased out the inhabitants of
the houses from the end of the street, the ones next to the ravine.
We went to live with my grandmother in Komsolskaia Street. Several children saw what happened. I remember one very hot day, we
had gone to the river to water the cows. There was such a stench!
There was what looked like blood flowing in the river, the water
was black, and smelt very bad. It was very hot. The Germans arrived in June. I don't know when they began shooting these people
but I know that it was very hot.

P.D.: **In your opinion, were the people in the trucks Jews?**

M.: You know, I couldn't see them like I can see you. In the beginning
they said that the people were exterminated, and then that they
were Jews and gypsies. I don't know if it was the truth because I
didn't go close.

P.D.: **Were the people who got down from the trucks silent or
were they shouting?**

M.: They threw them down from the trucks almost naked; there were grown-ups and little ones. But from the house we couldn't hear whether there were shouts. My father was also watching and he said to us "Oh, they have even thrown a child off the truck . . ." People kissed each other, and then the shooting began and they fell into the ravine. I don't think I was the only one to see it, but people are scared to say what they saw. I also want to tell you that that same year, or perhaps the winter of the following year, when we lived with my grandmother, bodies that were still intact were discovered. They hadn't had time to disintegrate. They brought prisoners of war who were imprisoned in the kolkhoze chicken farm. They had to open the pit, pour petrol on the bodies, and burn them.

P.D.: Did burning the bodies take a long time?

M.: Yes, it lasted a long time. As rich and cultivated as they were, they still forced the prisoners to collect the rings, earrings, and gold teeth. If they were so rich, why did they do that?! We were poor at the time, and yet we weren't the ones who took all those things. They also took the clothes on carts to a building that before the war had been a bank. I don't know where they sent them afterwards.

P.D.: Did they take the teeth and earrings from the people after they died?

M.: Yes, they took them after having burnt the bodies.

P.D.: Did they make the Russian prisoners do that?

M.: Yes. When we lived with my grandmother, the Germans also occupied that part of the town. One evening, we saw all the men on Sadovaia Street where we lived go out. Shouts and flames came from the chicken farm. The cries were terrible. They had poured petrol on it and burnt the prisoners of war alive. That is what I saw and heard. I am not the only one to have seen it.

P.D.: Did they come back that night?

M.: Yes. One evening, shortly after they had carried out that horror, my father came to see me and told me that the Germans were leaving. Very quickly, we went to see our houses that were next to the ravine. The place where it had all happened was empty. We were up high, where the Germans shot from, and we saw them leaving. It was morning, it was light and everything was empty and clean.

P.D.: Do you want to add anything?

M.: I remember that one day the German who lived with us came with all his clothes stained with red. He poured petrol on his undershirt because it was full of fleas. Afterwards he showed us on a map how far away the Russians were. Suddenly a soldier came in and shouted at him. They didn't want him to tell us all that. Shortly afterwards the Soviets arrived. I don't know what happened to the Germans.

P.D.: Thank you very much. Do you agree for your testimony to be put into the archives?

M.: Yes, but add nothing to what I have said. The Germans must see what their people did. They who were so cultivated and well brought up, look at what they did. What happened here was only a small drop in terms of everything they did in our country.

XVII

BUSK

Busk is a leafy little town made up of small neighborhoods bordering a winding and serene river, 70 kilometers from Lviv and Kiev. Before the war, it was a town in which Poles, Ukrainians, Jews, and Romanies all lived together. The majority of the town was Jewish and it had a magnificent Jewish cemetery, dotted with very ancient tombstones. In 1920, the French politician Georges Clemenceau came to Busk with a Viennese Jewish friend who wanted to find his father's tomb. If his description of this visit seems dated today, it nonetheless gives a sense of the Galician countryside, covered in mud, but also of the diversity of the inhabitants of Busk at the time.[1]

The Jewish community of Busk was long standing. The first synagogue in the town was built in 1502. In the nineteenth century, pious trends developed, notably the Hassidism of Belz[2] and Olesko, which became predominant. In 1921 a small Jewish school that taught Hebrew was founded.

The army of the Third Reich took possession of Busk on July 1, 1941, just 10 days after Germany's declaration of war on the Soviet Union. Busk was first run by a military governor. It was only in August of 1941 that it was given a civil administration. The town was integrated into the *Kreishauptmannschaft* Kamionka-Strumilowa, in the District of Galicia of the *Generalgouvernement* of Ukraine.[3] Busk was therefore subject to Kamionka-Strumilowa, a little neighboring town, itself under the *Generalgouvernement* of which the capital was Krakow.

Today, there is no longer a single Jew in Busk. All that remains is the cemetery where Clemenceau had taken his friend. The old synagogue, with its beautiful walls of newly-restored old white stone, has recently been allocated to an evangelical Christian community. It was in this town that we first decided to carry out our investigations. They spanned over three years.

We entered the little town of Busk for the first time on April 29, 2004. In the cool morning air we could make out, through the mud-splattered windows of our van, the central market where farmers, wrapped up in blue raincoats, sat on little wooden stools selling the produce from their farms. The bus station was full of parked small yellow buses with muddy windows that were waiting for passengers. We drove around in search of the town hall. It finally came into view, a small white building decorated with a blue and yellow flag, the symbol of the new state, at that point still under construction. We pushed open a heavy wooden door, the classic dreary Soviet colors emanated a sense of damp and cold. The signs on the offices did not seem to have benefited from the *glasnost* process. The mayor, a little man in a checked shirt open at the neck, very sober and efficient, received us for a few minutes. In his office, several green plants, sickly and pale, were trying to survive despite the lack of light. A little icon of Mary adorned one of the walls. He picked up the red plastic receiver of his telephone to call the land registry office. Several moments later, we were knocking on their door. An employee emerged from an office almost identical to that of the mayor, including the plants that seemed to be dying of boredom. The only difference was the telephone, which was green. Without asking any questions, she grabbed a coat made of imitation leopard fur which was hanging from a black metal coat stand. We left the building with her. She settled herself, without saying a word, in the front passenger seat of our van, and gave a brief order to the driver who silently started up the engine. After several minutes, I dared ask a question: "Where are we going?" "To Anna's," she replied.

The car stopped in Chevtchenko Street in front of a large grey building. Very clean white lace curtains were hanging at the windows. The land registry employee got out of the car, opened the green metal gate, went into the house, and came out two minutes later and sat back in the car. "She is going to come. We have to wait." I was already used to this silent efficiency which can seem harsh at first, but which often characterizes a job well done in Ukraine.

After 10 minutes or so, Anna appeared. She closed her door, blocking it with a nail. She had taken the time to smarten herself up. She came out, her forehead covered by a traditional multi-colored floral scarf from which a lock of grey hair escaped. Her low eyebrows and wrinkled forehead gave her a very determined air but her black eyes that darted around every which way betrayed her concern. Anna climbed into our van. We crossed a metal bridge that overhung an almost motionless small river that wound between green fields. She suddenly asked the driver to stop alongside one particular field; I spotted old Jewish tombstones, scattered here and there. It was the Jewish cemetery, or at least what remained of it. Many months later, a child showed us Jewish tombstones in a nearby field that were used to build a bridge for cows in a muddy spot. With the help of the village children we dismantled the "bridge for the cows" and took the stones one by one, on a long cart pulled by two horses, to the Jewish cemetery.

On this first visit, there were white goats, two brown horses, and a troop of geese milling around the tombs. One of the goats seemed to be posing proudly: it looked at us, stock still on a tombstone. Immediately, Anna jumped out of the van and raced alone down a little path of muddy earth that crossed the cemetery.

All the Ukrainian witnesses of the Holocaust we talked to, when brought back to the sites of the Jews' assassination, had made their own way, without waiting for us, with rapid steps toward the scene of the crime, as though overtaken by the vision of those men and women who had been there during those wretched days. A vision that has never left them. I heard her murmuring: "Yes, there, there! They were taken there . . . They forced them to run by beating them, even elderly people. Some of them found it hard to walk." As she moved, she recaptured the memory of the child who saw the massacre of her Jewish neighbors. "They were brought to the door of the cemetery in a car from the ghetto. Some were already dead." She reached the lower ground, on the bank of the river, and stopped, then suddenly began speaking again, as though in a single breath: "It is here that the Jews had to undress completely and place their clothes on the ground. They threw their jewels in the river so that the Germans couldn't collect them when they were forced to undress! The Germans were furious. Afterwards they forced them to take off their clothes further away from the river, down there!" She climbed, a little out of breath, onto a long slope covered in grass. "Under my feet, just there, they shot them one by one, with a bullet from behind." With her right hand she pointed to the nape of her neck, looking at us to be sure that she was understood. It seemed impossible to imagine that this bucolic landscape was the backdrop to such a massacre. She was talking about her experiences for the first time since 1943. Several times she mentioned a memory of her childhood friend, a young Jew from the ghetto. He was taken by the police to this field with all his family. He knew that Anna was watching the execution, hidden with her friends in a hay barn. This barn, very close by, behind the Jewish cemetery, was made of uneven planks through which she could watch. Anna was 14. He was pushed far from the others who were waiting, standing in front of the pit with his family, stripped of all their clothes. Just before the shooting, he had turned toward Anna and made her a little hand gesture as if to say goodbye, and then shouted "Farewell life!" Then the assassins started shooting.

My heart tightened. For more than 60 years, Anna had kept inside herself the last words of her childhood friend whose life was stolen from him. What a delicate task, to receive the last words of a Jewish child eliminated by young men who had come from Germany to build a "superior race"! As Israel Singer, the former chairman of the World Jewish Congress said to me once: "Finally, you are bearing the words of the dead." If I have done all this research, it is for the sake of these children who were assassinated in cold blood. I left Busk with a heavy heart. That evening, in the blue van with muddy windows, everyone was silent, alone with their thoughts.

We left Busk determined to come back to continue the investigation after scouring the German and Soviet archives for information.

We came back on May 5, 2005. It was raining over Busk. We had to keep wiping the condensation off the windshield to see where we were going. The uniformity of the landscape and the absence of signposts added to the difficulty of our journey along chaotic roads. We had to keep stopping to ask the way. When Micha asked someone for directions, he always got the same rapid response: "*Priamo*"—straight ahead, which usually meant that the person did not know. We finally arrived at the Jewish cemetery, which looked very grey under the curtain of rain. We had gone back to see Anna but she was no longer there, or rather, we were told, she no longer wished to give us her testimony. All her neighbors had harassed her, thinking that we had given her money for talking to us. Money and Jews, Jews and money. I am very familiar with this kind of association. These clichés often lead insidiously to hatred and violence.

Under the downpour, I glimpsed a limping shepherd wearing a large dark green plastic cape, like those worn by soldiers. He appeared to be pursuing his ill-disciplined herd of five black and white cows that wanted to graze at length on the tufts of grass that grew between the Jewish tombstones. From the car, Micha shouted: "Do you know Anna?" He turned and looked up, curious, and asked why we were looking for her. We explained our investigation to him. His eyes widened and lit up under his cap of grey, sodden material. He replied: "I was with Anna in the barn on the day of the shooting. There were five of us children there." He had seen everything and agreed to speak, there in the cemetery, under the rain. We frequently met witnesses on a street corner. But every encounter was accompanied by a sense of astonishment.

In a few minutes, we had gotten out our large black umbrellas, the microphone, and the camera to interview this gentleman, called Anton Davidovski. As he started, he seemed very agitated. He tried, with jerky, disordered gestures, to indicate to us that the Jews had fallen head first into the pit, and that the gunmen, the Ukrainian police, were standing with rifles beside German officers. The interview was very mobile since the cows were running hither and thither; he repeatedly interrupted his testimony to regroup them with the aid of his stick. I ended up looking after the little herd myself. This huge field, in which cows were feeding contentedly under the shower of rain, was the site of the large mass graves of the Jews assassinated in Busk. Anton saw numerous carts transporting Jews who had died in the ghetto pass in front of his door: "They had already killed a lot of Jews in the ghetto of Busk. The Germans had requisitioned peasants with their carts to transport the Jews who had died in the ghetto to the pit. My cousin was one of them. Me, I saw everything!" All through his testimony he continually repeated, like a moan or a haunted suffering: "You don't treat people like that. One wouldn't even treat wood like that. Their heads were dragging on the ground."

One of his neighbors, a Polish woman, had hidden a Jewish woman in her hay barn whom she employed as a seamstress. One day the Germans had come into the street to see if there were still Jews hiding there. The Polish woman had come out of her house shouting *"Jude! Jude!"* A German had come into the yard. He had killed the Jewish woman with a bullet to the head with his pistol and had left the body in the middle of the hay barn.

Anton went on with this story, his eyes lowered. "The Germans kept 30 or so very pretty Jewish women that they put to work in the offices of the Gestapo but whom they also used as 'sex objects' for the police and the Germans." He explained that these women were not killed in Busk but 5 kilometers away, in a forest. When the Germans had left the town, the Jewish women had all been pregnant. The Germans in Busk hadn't had the courage to kill them themselves. They had called on another commando, from nearby Sokal, to assassinate them.

This story was confirmed to us a year later, on August 30, 2006, when we meet Polina, a woman who lived in Chuchmani, a little hamlet six kilometers from Busk, not far from the forest where the Jewish girls were executed. "There were shootings in the forest. I didn't see but people told me about it. For example, the Jewish girls who worked for the *Kommandantur,* bringing food or cooking for them—I don't know which—were killed in the forest where a pit had been dug. I knew them because at that time I taught at the supply center." The Jewish women selected by the Germans as sex slaves and assassinated at the end of the war are not mentioned in any of the archives. Yet witnesses often mentioned them. They knew them before the occupation and were often present at their assassination. The Holocaust of Jewish women in Eastern Europe constitutes a chapter of history that has barely been opened.

Anton walked further into the field and showed us, one by one, the communal graves of the Jews as he remembered. He seemed to not notice the rain as he walked, calmly counting: "One, two, three . . . seven. Yes, seven graves." I ran after him, trying to shelter him from the rain with an umbrella.

During our investigations in Busk, we met numerous other witnesses.

Eugenia, was the daughter of the village violinist. He had played the violin for the Jews before the war, for the Germans during the war, and for the Ukrainians after the end of the German occupation. He knew Yiddish folk music, Bavarian dances, and traditional Galician songs all equally well. He had died a short time before and had wanted to be buried with his violin. Eugenia talked about her father with much emotion.

I met her in the courtyard of the family farm. It was obvious that they were very poor. Animals, particularly chickens and geese, milled about all over the place. The ground of the earthen courtyard was littered with abandoned objects—worn-out agricultural machines, a crib, chipped vases. We looked for a clean seat for her to sit on. Eventually I found a tree stump on which we placed a sheet. She sat down, her eyes looking about keenly, happy to reveal what she saw.

During her whole testimony, her sister sat behind her, immobile in front of the camera, holding in her hands the portrait of their father with his violin. Eugenia remembered life with the Jews of Busk. She told us with much joy how, every Saturday, for Shabbat, she would go to the Havners, some Jewish friends, for whom she fulfilled the function of *shabbes goy.*⁴ "When I was small, I went to light the fire at their home on Saturday. It was a holiday for them. They gave us matches because they didn't have the right to use them, and we lit the fire to cook large loaves of bread." The Germans knew her father well because of his music. He was requisitioned by the *deisatnik*⁵ of their street to dig the big pit, and to fill it in after the shootings. Her mother was very worried when she saw the *desiatnik* taking him away. She took her daughter Eugenia to the other side of the river, next to the wooden church, to check what the Germans were going to do with her husband. But she couldn't stay with her daughter because the tufts of grass were not high enough to hide an adult. So only the child saw the preparation of the pits, the arrival of the Jews, their assassination, and the filling in of the pits. She explained: "From where I was sitting, I couldn't see the Jews and the gunmen very clearly; there were so many people all around." Listening to her, I understood that the civilians requisitioned on the days of the execution were sometimes more numerous than the assassins and their victims. I asked her what her father said when he got back that evening. "He said that the pit had not been big enough. They were going to have to dig another one the following day."

When we knocked for the first time at the gate of Stepan David-ovski's house, he was busy preparing a meal. He had just slit the throat of a chicken, and he was holding the bleeding animal in one hand, ready to be plucked. He asked us to come back the following morning.

The day after, at exactly 9 o'clock, all our little team had gathered outside his door. He talked to us for a long time, seated in a large brown armchair in the middle of an enormous room that was luminous and clean. His memory was prodigious. The son of a Greek Catholic deacon, he had grown up in a culture that considerably increased the precision of his memories. He particularly remembered the daily life of the Jews, in-cluding their surnames: "They lived in the center of town and in the streets outside of the center as well. In Kievskaia Street, for instance, lived Pavel Koval. He made packaging for bottles. In Shachkevitch Street there was another Jew, Nioukhim, who was a farmer. He had a plot of land and cows. Yet another Jew, Havner, had a shop. There was also Chmul, who sold milk. There were Jews in all the villages." He remembered the *Judenrat*,[6] the creation of the Jewish police, Jews being forced to live in the ghetto, and to wear an armband with a star. He saw the ghetto work squads leaving every day to work on the roads accompanied by Jewish po-lice and German soldiers. Stepan himself had worked in the ghetto, in a lemonade factory. He had cleaned the empty bottles, filled them with lemonade, and delivered them. The ghetto was "open" but that did not mean that one could circulate freely in it. Stepan came and went for his work, equipped with a *Kennkarte*[7] that he would present in case of an identity check. He showed it to us, proud of having preserved it so care-fully. All that is missing is the photograph. He knew all the administrative workings of the town during the war, the relations between the *Judenrat* and the *Kommandantur* and between the *Judenrat,* the Jewish police, the *Shutzpolizei*[8] and the *Feldgendarmerie,* the offices of which were set up in the Ukrainian barracks. Most of the walls that housed the German administrations remain intact today. The buildings were used for other purposes as soon as the German occupation was over. Stepan also knew the precise number of Germans present in the town: 300.

Never, in the whole of Ukraine, had I met a witness with such acute perception and who could offer such a detailed account of the whole town's history and geography, and of the ghetto under Nazi occupation. He told us in detail about the events of the great *Aktion*[9] of 1943.

On the morning of April 16, 2006 I went to pray in the Latin Armenian church of Lviv. The crowd of believers was dense, even early in the morning. Svetlana always accompanied me to church. She often placed a beeswax candle before an icon. Without these moments of recollection and celebration, we would not have been able to keep going. The sun was shining but the air was cool. It was Palm Sunday, in a week, it would be Easter.

Back in Busk, many people were not able to enter the Greek Catholic church with their beautiful highly decorated palms. The latecomers were outside, listening in silence to the account of the passion of Christ. Children were wearing their smartest clothes. We were celebrating Jesus's entry into Jerusalem. The affable priest had asked us to be present at this mass, during which he was going to announce that we were trying to find out how the Jews were killed, here in Busk, 63 years ago. When we contacted him, he had replied: "It is only right that the Jews should have a tomb. Our bishop himself, saved many Jews during the war. I will do everything I can to help you. Come to the Palm Sunday mass; a lot of people will be there. You will be able to meet those who saw the executions."

The children came out first, happily running and jumping about, a blessed palm in their hand. A large, austere wooden cross stood at the entrance to the church. It had been decorated for the holiday with a large crown of green boxwood. As soon as the mass was over, we were approached by a horde of elderly people, mainly women. Witnesses who saw the ghetto and the executions of the Jews streamed out of the mass one after the other. A small throng formed in front of us. There were so many that we could not possibly interview them all. Svetlana took a note of their names and addresses on the blank pages of a little diary.

How moving this was: All these Ukrainians who, alerted a few minutes earlier by the parish priest, cut short the Palm Sunday holiday so that the truth about the genocide of the Jews could be known and communicated.

One of these people, dressed all in black, a mantilla fixed to a little round black hat, was absolutely determined to speak. She continued to repeat: "I saw everything, I saw everything!" She finally made her way through the crowd and came up to us. Her name was Lydia.

Her family practiced the same profession as mine: butchering animals and selling them in a shop. As traders, they had numerous encounters with the owners of the Jewish shops in the center of town. Every witness saw part of the genocide. None of them can recount the whole thing. That is the limit of visual memory. Lydia saw horse-drawn carts bearing the bodies of Jewish women killed in the ghetto. She believed that these women had been hiding or tried to escape. She remembered having run behind these carts full of bodies as a child, all the way to the door of the cemetery. She supposed that the Germans had killed a lot of people in the ghetto. She also saw trucks full of women and Jewish children, who were crying.

Lydia followed all our investigations in town. But it was only much later that she would finally say what she really saw, encouraged by her daughter who kept telling her: "Mama, you must tell the whole truth!" One day she arrived without warning in the Jewish cemetery, and showed us where all the communal graves were.

We also met a civil engineer who had been given the task, after the war, of recycling the houses of the Jews; she told us that she found bank notes and candlesticks. We also found people who came at night to give food to the Jews of the ghetto in exchange for clothes. Lydia told us how people could get into the ghetto without getting caught by the guards.

In addition to gathering testimonies on the ground, we continued with our research in the Soviet archives at the Holocaust Memorial Museum in Washington D.C. There, far from the geese and horses of Busk, in the peace and quiet of the research center, we spent hours sitting in front of microfilm readers. We found several names of other Ukrainian witnesses from Busk who had given evidence in 1944 to the town district attorney.[10] The Soviet archives are proportionate to the size of the country they come from: 16 million pages. In 1944, the district attorney of Busk had interrogated Ukrainian witnesses who lived in Chevtchenko Street, that long street that bordered the Jewish cemetery. Without realizing it, in 2006 we had knocked at the same doors as the district attorney did 62 years earlier.

The degree to which the testimonies dovetailed with each other was astounding, in terms of both form and content. The Jewish cemetery had had a caretaker, Yvan, before the war. His house next to the cemetery at 13 Chevtchenko Street no longer exists. When I read his testimony contained in the archives I discovered that he not only recounted the same facts as Anton but that the very tone of his narrative

was similar: "The Ukrainian police and four to five Germans transported, for over a week, Jews in a truck to a pit that had already been
dug. The naked Jews had to sit down in front of the pit, facing it, and
they were killed with machine guns. They killed a lot of Jews; I don't
know how many. All the Jews are buried in 10 or more pits next to the
Jewish cemetery in Busk. I know all these pits."

We found the testimony of a cleaning lady who worked for the Germans. She heard them talking about the executions every evening. Her
testimony is the most complete because she remembered all the executions, with their dates and circumstances. She recounted in particular
that the Germans came back every evening, very proud of what they
had done, boasting about it.

Her neighbor, Stanislav, lived at number 25 Chevtchenko Street. He
was a *desiatnik*. Most of the witnesses that had been requisitioned in
Busk to assist the Germans in the execution of the Jews stated that it
had been the *desiatnik* who had come to take them from their homes,
under the orders of the mayor. In Busk, the assassins from the Reich
used the Soviet structure for the requisitions. In his testimony,
Stanislav clearly named Lehner, the head of the German gendarmerie,
as the one who had taken charge of the executions. He said: "During
the German occupation, I worked as a *desiatnik* in Busk, in
Chevtchenko Street. In May 1943, I don't remember the exact date,
German gendarmes came to my house on the orders of Lieutenant
Ludwig Lehner who was head of the German gendarmerie, and also
German commander of the town of Busk. These German gendarmes
demanded, under threat of death, that I bring citizens to dig pits near
the Jewish cemetery. Under that threat, I followed the orders and when
the pits were ready, a German gendarme by the name of Maier and
other German gendarmes and Ukrainian police transported the Jews

from the ghetto to the pits where they were forced to undress completely. They had to put their things in a pile and, in groups of 10 or more people, they had to kneel before the pits. Then they were killed with machine guns. The executions lasted more than a week. More than a thousand Jews were killed before the eyes of the citizens, but we couldn't approach the pits. Then the citizens and I, as *desiatnik*, were forced to bury the bodies in the pits . . . In total, in the Jewish cemetery there are almost 10 pits where the bodies of the Jews were buried."

We could have ended things there. The simple comparison between the oral memory we had gathered in the area in 2006, and the testimony recoded by the district attorney of Busk in 1944 was enough to confirm our certainty and our knowledge of the execution of the Jewish community of Busk. But an unexpected event turned around and enriched our investigation.

Jacques Fredj, the director of the Holocaust Memorial in Paris, had long expressed the desire for archaeological research to be carried out on an extermination site, so that no one could object that we didn't have material proof. I thought the idea a good one but difficult to implement. To my knowledge, no archaeological research on a mass grave had been carried out since 1990.[11] I then decided, with my team, to organize an expert study in Busk. Why Busk? Because the inhabitants had told us that the graves had never been tampered with. They agreed that all the houses in the villages had a "view" of the graves, and so since the war no marauder had dared to open them in search of gold.

We decided we would insist on the presence of an orthodox rabbi so that the excavations would not contravene Jewish law. The son of Rabbi Meshi Zahav, the founder of Zaka,[12] accepted to come from Jerusalem in person to oversee the work in its entirety. I called on the dean of the archaeology department in Lviv because I wanted the work to be carried out by an Ukrainian organization. The excavations were organized in August 2006 and were to last three weeks with the help of archaeologists.

The challenge was doubly complex. On the one hand we had to respect Jewish laws and on the other we wanted to obtain scientific results as precise as possible in terms of the identity of the victims, their number, and the cause of death. The Jewish law, the *Halakha,* specifies that bodies must not be moved under any circumstance, particularly the victims of the Holocaust. According to Orthodox Jewish tradition, these victims are resting in the fullness of God, and any movement of their bodies would disturb that peace. Hence the archaeologist could only uncover the first layer of bodies, taking care not to move any bones. In addition, the bodies had to be covered up again as soon as the archaeologist finished working. Svetlana therefore spent the month of August not interpreting but looking in all the textile shops in the area for white sheets that she bought every day by the dozen, so as to be able to respect that tradition.

We thought that in Busk there were at most seven communal graves. When the archaeologist began inspecting the relief of the terrain, he estimated the number of communal graves at 17. This was not even the site of the execution of all the Jews of Busk who were assassinated by the Reich. Busk is situated not far from Poland and the ghetto was the target of various German *Aktions.*[13] A large part of the Jewish community was taken by train to the extermination camp at Belzec, in present-day Poland. The graves therefore contained only the last Jews of Busk, around 1,750 people. Most of them were women and children who had hidden after the German attacks on the ghetto. They were found in cellars, imprisoned in the gendarmerie, and then shot.[14]

The bodies appeared one after the other. We were able to establish whether it was a man, a woman, or a child and above all the cause of death. The impact of the bullets and the position of the bodies showed that they had all been shot and buried alive. Many of the women's bodies were found holding a baby, to protect it from the flow of sand. It was three weeks of macabre discoveries.

Before we arrived, the villagers had used the green, flowered fields over the pits for their geese and horses to graze in peace. Our undertaking involved numerous negotiations. A couple of farmers were in the habit of crossing the village with their cows, passing through the Jewish cemetery and the site of the communal graves. They came one evening to ask us politely if they could continue to pass through there, otherwise they would have to take a long detour. I devised a pathway through the communal graves so that every morning and evening, at milking time, men and animals could pass.

Of course the site also had to be guarded at night because many of the dead still had gold teeth and all too often the inhabitants of the village would come to ask us the same question: "Have you found gold?"

After three weeks, all the graves had been opened. It was impossible to carry out a typical scientific study because we had to respect Jewish law and not move any of the bones. We could therefore only observe what appeared on the surface. The missing information, though, appears in the German and Soviet archives of 1944, which explicitly mention the execution of the Jews in the cemetery. These were also confirmed for us by our 10 witnesses, who identified the grave sites with precision.

This research was very difficult to undertake, particularly because of the indifference of the village people. A single villager came, dressed in black, with a little bunch of red and yellow flowers from her garden.

She placed it on one of the mass graves and then withdrew a little and stood in silence for a while. She left without saying anything.

Before closing the graves again, I hired a helicopter (the one that monitored the oil pipelines crossing the region) to take aerial shots of the ensemble of graves. When I saw the helicopter land, I thought that only its paintwork looked recent. There were no seatbelts. Undeterred, Guillaume climbed into the helicopter without hesitation. Thanks to this means of transport, we were able to measure the extent of the massacre: 17 graves next to the Jewish cemetery, which seemed very small in comparison to them. I imagine that if we could open all the mass graves we would have to take aerial photos of the whole of Ukraine. A mass cemetery of anonymous pits into which men, women, and children were thrown. Not a camp but a country of graves.

Once the archeological study was finished, we had to cover these graves with a particular kind of tar used for airport runways so that the dead would not be disturbed in their rest by people looking for dental gold. The assistant mayor of Rawa-Ruska, Yaroslav, came to our aid by coordinating the work.

On September 1, 2006, after the graves were finally covered, the great rabbi of the yeshiva of Belz, Rabbi Bohl, arrived from Lviv in a grey car, accompanied by 10 young members of his religious community to recite the *kaddish*.[15]

> *Yitgadal veyitkadach chemé raba*
> *Bealma di vera khiroute.*[16]

The unchanging words seemed to resonate and take us back to a time when, long ago, the *kaddish* must have been recited often. Despite the constant difficulties, I had astonishingly felt nothing during the whole excavation. But when the *kaddish* resounded through the Jewish cemetery, before the communal graves that had been forgotten and denied since 1943, my emotions spilled over. For the first time in a very long time, I had the feeling that the boat was coming into harbor. Finally, a Jewish prayer was being pronounced for these young mothers and these little Jewish children who had been killed and buried like animals beside the river.

On the morning of September 2, 2006, we left Busk, moved and tired. For three weeks we had been shuttling every day between the hotel and the graves. Early in the morning—the landscape was already filled with fog although August was just over—we went back and, for the last time, looked at the 17 grave sites. We were surprised to see several locals, whom we had barely seen before then, moving up the slope with wheelbarrows, on their way to collect the leftover bags of cement.

Stepan Davidovski, Busk, region of Lviv, August 25, 2006
Patrick Desbois: What did your parents do?
Stepan Davidovski: My father was a deacon here in Busk for 35 years. He also cultivated his land. He owned horses . . .
P.D.: Were you at school when the war began?
S.D.: I had almost finished school in 1939. I was in seventh grade.
P.D.: Can you describe the arrival of the Germans into the town. Was there fighting?
S.D.: When the Germans arrived, the NKVD[17] had already escaped. They had summarily shot 33 people in the prisons: doctors and engineers. Then they left. Their families could bury them when the

Germans arrived, directly from Lviv. Everything became theirs. They destroyed the old town and established their power.

P.D.: Was the ghetto created immediately on the Germans' arrival or afterwards?

S.D.: It wasn't created straight away. In the beginning, the Jews continued living in their houses and working, taking care of their affairs. That was also the case in the other villages. In the autumn, two ghettoes were built but the Jews of neighboring towns continued living there. They announced to the Jewish population that they were going to live in a special residence zone, in a ghetto, and that the Jews should go to such and such a building in such and such a ghetto. The streets were guarded, barred, and 20 or 30 people lived in each room. They were hungry and suffering from typhus. They weren't free any more.

P.D.: How were the Jewish police created?

S.D.: There was a *Judenrat* in the ghetto that was ordered to create its own police, the *Judenpolizei*,[18] to maintain order and to take the Jews to work . . . They were around 20 policemen.

P.D.: Did the Jews have to wear the star straight away?

S.D.: They had to put an armband with a star from the first days of the ghetto. They had to make it themselves. They were allowed to go only where they were authorized, otherwise they were shot on the spot.

P.D.: Did they send the Jews to work just in businesses? Solely inside the ghetto?

S.D.: In general it was for work such as digging ditches or loading up trains in railway stations. Everything was organized. They were accompanied by soldiers and Jewish police who had batons. It was all done German-style.

P.D.: Did you have an *Ausweis*[19] to go in and out of the ghetto?

S.D.: Yes, I had a *kennkarte*. There was no guard at the entry to the ghetto but if a German stopped me and asked me what I was doing in the ghetto, I showed him this paper. There was no one at the entrance; the Jews knew that they shouldn't go out or they would be killed.

P.D.: Could the Jews buy food outside?

S.D.: They couldn't buy items freely. It occurred in secret. People brought food and exchanged it for other things. I myself took food to Jews who were poor.

P.D.: Were there *Volksdeutsche* in Busk before the war?

S.D.: Before the war, the word *Volksdeutsche* didn't exist. One simply said "Germans." They were German "settlers." In 1940, after the Ribbentrop-Molotov agreement, they were repatriated to Germany. The *Volksdeutsche* were not real Germans. They were Poles and Ukrainians who had German names. The Germans then said they were *Volksdeutsche*.

P.D.: Did these *Volksdeutsche* have links with German soldiers or not necessarily?

S.D.: No. They were simple farmers or workers. They didn't think of themselves as Germans. We helped them a bit by giving them food because they had been reclassified as *Volksdeutsche*. That is all. They didn't have a link with the Germans; it was just the Germans who considered them *Volksdeutsche* because they had German names.

P.D.: Were the Jews of the ghetto religious? Were there communists?

S.D.: There were communists among them. They were already communist under Poland. Most of those who belonged to the communist party or the communist youth had left for the east before the arrival of the Germans with Soviet troops. Those who stayed, Jews and non-Jews, were shot by the Germans two or three days after their arrival.

P.D.: When did the first action in the ghetto begin?

S.D.: In 1943, in mid-June. It was a mass action. One day, at 7 in the morning, they announced to the *Judenrat* and to Jewish families that they had to gather at the marketplace. I don't know whether they told them it was for some kind of call or to check papers but in any event it was a trick. Once they were in the marketplace, the gendarmes and the police surrounded them. Of course, some of them must have hidden in cellars or escaped somewhere. Those who tried to escape from the marketplace were killed. Then they were loaded onto trucks and taken to the forest of Rabovi, I don't know exactly where. They were shot there. They were also taken to the forest of Chuchmani, others to Sokal, and Rawa-Ruska. There were too many of them. Those who were hiding in the houses, cellars, and fields were caught by the Germans. Each time they caught between 10 and 15 people. They were brought here, forced to dig a pit with spades, undress, and were shot. They kept a few to fill in the pit. That went on all summer.

P.D.: Did these killings go on every day and every week?

S.D.: It depended. They caught some one day then, sometimes, three days later they caught others, sometimes a week later . . .

P.D.: They caught them, gathered them in the prison and when there were enough of them, took them to the cemetery, didn't they?

S.D.: Yes, they made groups of 10 or 15 people. The Germans also kept the Jews to do certain work. Young girls, for example, they kept for themselves. Later on they killed them, they didn't let anyone stay alive.

P.D.: Did the Germans requisition all the goods that the Jews had?

S.D.: Of course, they took everything. They were not going to hand them out to the villagers.

P.D.: Did the Jewish police remain until the end of the ghetto?

S.D.: Yes. They weren't shot. They were sent to the ghetto of Olesko, where the police were sent.

P.D.: Were the *Judenrat* kept after the action?

S.D.: The *Judenrat* had no privileges. They were treated like the others.

P.D.: Was there a hospital in the ghetto?

S.D.: Of course not. There was never a hospital for anyone.

P.D.: Did the Jewish police have particular rights?

S.D.: They had food rations and clothes. They could go from one ghetto to the other.

P.D.: Could they go into the town?

S.D.: Yes. They could even escape. Thirty or 40 Jews spent the whole war in the forest. Some people hid Jews in their home. A family that lived quite near hid Jews. One of them went into the ghetto one day and was caught by the Germans, who asked him where he had been hiding; he told them. They shot him, as well as a woman, and another man, Jews who were hiding with him, and they sent those who had hid them to a concentration camp.

P.D.: Were the women and children of the ghetto killed at a particular time?

S.D.: They didn't separate people. They were all gathered at the marketplace at the same time.

P.D.: We found a communal grave with only women and children; does that mean they were killed separately?

S.D.: If women were with their children and they caught them in the fields, or else women who were hiding with their children, they killed them together.

P.D.: Were Ukrainians requisitioned to collect the Jews' clothes after the action?

S.D.: The Germans had already taken what they wanted of the Jews' possessions. The Germans ordered the destruction of the wooden buildings of the ghetto. They asked the Jews to give them so many clothes, so much money, so much gold . . . and they stored them. Bit by bit, they took all their goods.

P.D.: Did the mayor of Busk have to account to the Germans?

S.D.: He did only what the Germans said. He had a limited power.

Eugenia Nazarenko, Busk, region of Lviv, August 22, 2006
Eugenia had wanted to talk for a long time. She played the triangle alongside her father who played the violin. She knew Jewish tunes.

Patrick Desbois: Did you see what happened to the Jews in the cemetery?

Eugenia Nazarenko: I saw everything that happened.

P.D.: They let you pass?

E.N.: I was able to get to the river. After that there were a lot of police. My father didn't even see me from where he was. The Jews dug the pits and it was our people who filled them in because no one was left to do it . . . The Germans asked the *desiatniki* to gather our men to do it. If they didn't go, they shot them.

P.D.: How did you know something was happening down there?

E.N.: Everyone knew that they were killing Jews. In every village they made a ghetto, put all the Jews in it, then killed them.

P.D.: What did you see from where you were?

E.N.: I was little, I didn't understand everything that was going on. I saw that there were a lot of people, Germans, Ukrainians who had been requisitioned to fill in the pits because the Germans were not going to do that.

P.D.: How did the Jews come into the cemetery? From the large gate?

E.N.: They brought them on the big road, which was already asphalted, in trucks, in carts and on foot. However they could—they had to do it as quickly as possible.

P.D.: Were there several days of executions?

E.N.: I cannot tell you. In fact, they dug a first pit which they filled in the first day. After, they dug another. It didn't happen in a single day. Afterwards they killed the people they hadn't succeeded in shooting on another day.

P.D.: Did the Jews have to undress before being killed?

E.N.: Those who were wearing good clothes had to take them off; the others were thrown in dressed. Not all of them got undressed.

P.D.: Were they killed one by one or in groups?

E.N.: They placed them around the pit, shot them and they fell in the pit. And so on. They all fell in the pit, they were in such hysteria. Some fell when they weren't even dead. I remember a woman who managed to get out of the pit; she took refuge with another woman from the village. The woman denounced her and the Jewish woman was caught and killed.

P.D.: How many days did the killings go on for?

E.N.: It didn't last long. What went on for a long time was the period they were kept in the ghetto. They were told that they were going to be allowed to live. But in the end they were all killed.

P.D.: Are you talking about the Jewish police?

E.N.: Yes. They were a sort of police, they had batons. They thought that they were going to be allowed to live. They stayed alive quite a long time but at a certain time, the order to kill them was given.

P.D.: Were the police also killed in the cemetery?

E.N.: Yes. In the same pit. First they brought the civilians, then the police.

P.D.: Did you see the execution of the Jewish police?

E.N.: I didn't see it myself; it was people of the village who talked about it. They killed all the Jews, they weren't going to let them live. The Germans here said they wouldn't kill them but they received the order to kill all the Jews. They had an order from on high.

P.D.: Was there a leader who gave the order to shoot?

E.N.: Certainly. There had to be a leader.

P.D.: Did you hear someone giving an order before each shot?

E.N.: I didn't hear. I heard simply "bang, bang, bang." The people were around the pit, I don't know how many they were—three, four, five . . . They shot them and they fell into the pit.

P.D.: Did they kill the children or throw them alive into the pit?

E.N.: No, they shot everybody. They were all killed together. The mothers were carrying their children in their arms. If I had been in their place, I would have wanted to die with my child. They brought them all together. Perhaps they shot people who tried to escape along the way. But Ukrainians must have buried them because that was what was done. They were human beings like me and you.

P.D.: Did your father come back late at night?

E.N.: No, it was still light. They took the Jews quite early in the morning.

P.D.: Did the Germans like music?

E.N.: Yes, my father played them German music and dances. He was a good musician. It was how he earned a living.

P.D.: Did the Germans like dancing?

E.N.: And how! They danced German dances.

P.D.: Did the Germans like to amuse themselves in the evening or during the day?

E.N.: Day and night, whenever they could. It depended on their days off.

P.D.: During the German occupation was there an official visit of Germans asking for music and a banquet?

E.N.: No. They only went to the café. There were not just Germans there but also Ukrainians, guards.

P.D.: On the day of the executions, did the Germans bother your father because they knew him?

E.N.: No one remembered him. They were busy with the execution. They took people, shot them, buried them, all as quickly as possible.

P.D.: Was there a party the evening of the execution, as there was in some villages?

E.N.: No. There were not very many of them here. They didn't stay here very long. They had to go to Moscow.

P.D.: Did the Germans take the time to eat and drink during the execution?

E.N.: No. They did nothing but kill and bury people. Afterwards they left. I don't know if they had a party afterwards.

P.D.: Did the Germans keep Jewish women?

E.N.: No, they killed them all, one after the other.

P.D.: Did the Germans leave the clothes or did they take them in trucks?

E.N.: They left them for the people of the village. The villagers were poor. Those who didn't have enough to clothe their children took them.

P.D.: Did the Germans burn something?

E.N.: No. They filled in the pits and that's all. Then they left.

P.D.: Was there a guardian at night?

E.N.: No. They killed them and left. If someone fell into the pit alive he perhaps managed to get out of the pit. Everyone was all mixed up in the pit: children, old people . . .

P.D.: Was it sunny the day of the execution?

E.N.: It wasn't raining. On the other hand, I couldn't tell you what time it was or what month. I think it might have been spring.

P.D.: Did your father tell you what had happened that evening?

E.N.: Yes. Everyone cried when he told what had happened. There was me, my mother, and my two sisters. I also had a sister who spent two years in Germany. The day she came back, my father was wounded in the finger by the Gestapo. My sister went to the Gestapo to know what they had done to my father. The Germans were surprised because she spoke German. They wondered if she was a spy but she showed them a document that showed that she was working in Germany and that she was on holiday. That was how my father was freed.

P.D.: Was your father requisitioned another time by the *desiatnik?*

E.N.: Yes. My mother went to see this *desiatnik* and she slapped his face, saying to him "Why are you requisitioning him? He is wounded."

P.D.: Was this *desiatnik* Ukrainian?

E.N.: Yes, like us.

P.D.: Was he a *desiatnik* before the war?

E.N.: No. He was a lowlife, that's all.

P.D.: Did you go into the ghetto?

E.N.: Yes, my elder sister worked there. I don't really know what she did. But she didn't stay long because afterwards they sent her to Germany.

P.D.: Was the ghetto closed?

E.N.: No, there were just the Jewish police who guarded the Jews. They didn't let anyone in.

P.D.: Did the Jews try to buy food outside?

E.N.: You know, our people, the Ukrainians, tried to take them food. They were people like us, we had grown up together, our parents knew their parents. We lived together, we did our shopping in their shops. The Ukrainians liked the Jews. They were good people. I remember my mother had sold a plot of land to a Jew for him to build his shop on. When I was little, we went to steal eggs there, to buy ourselves sweets.

P.D.: Do you remember the name of this shopkeeper?

E.N.: Havner. I don't remember his first name. When I was little, I went to light the fire at their house on Saturdays. It was a holiday for them. They gave us matches because they weren't allowed to use them and we lit the fire to bake a large loaf of bread.

P.D.: Did Mr. Havner have children?

E.N.: Yes, he had a son and a daughter, Gousia. That was why my father called me Gousia.

P.D.: Were they all killed?

E.N.: Of course. They were all killed.

P.D.: Were they killed the day of the big execution?

E.N.: Yes, they were all killed at the same time. First they were assembled in the ghetto, all of them, to the very last person. Havner had asked my grandfather to sell him his land for him to build his shop on. He sold his produce and he even gave us things when we didn't have money. We were poor.

P.D.: **Did you see Mr. Havner the day of the execution?**

E.N.: No. They stayed a long time in the ghetto—six months, perhaps longer.

P.D.: **Were you able to get food to them when they were in the ghetto?**

E.N.: No. I don't know where they were in the ghetto. We were frightened to approach it.

P.D.: **How did they announce to the Jews that they had to go into the ghetto? By notices?**

E.N.: No, there were no notices. Most of our Jews lived in the center; the center was Jewish. They had their shops there. Very few were farmers, perhaps just one or two in our street, not more.

P.D.: **Was the synagogue in the ghetto?**

E.N.: No. It was in the same place as it is today.

P.D.: **Did the Germans burn or destroy the synagogue?**

E.N.: They used it as a warehouse, like the Russians.

P.D.: **Were the Havners and the Jews you knew religious?**

E.N.: Yes. They put these little boxes on their heads every Saturday. When they prayed, you couldn't disturb them.

P.D.: **Did these Jews speak Ukrainian?**

E.N.: Yes, they spoke Ukrainian like we are doing. They spoke Ukrainian very well. On the other hand, in their homes, during celebrations, they spoke in their language. If they didn't want you to understand what they were saying, they spoke in their language.

P.D.: Thank you very much. Do you agree for your testimony to be placed in the archives and made public in museums and universities?

E.N.: Yes. I have told you what I know and haven't told you what I don't know.

XVIII

HE WHO SAVES A SINGLE LIFE
SAVES THE WHOLE WORLD

During our research we also met individuals or families who had saved Jews. Many of them had been denounced, and tortured. Some of these family members had been shot.

I remember particularly Galina Boulavka, whose mother Anna had come back from St. Petersburg very ill. She wanted to die in her home, in her native town of Lubomil near the Polish border.

One day in April 2007, when we were looking for witnesses in the market, Galina came up to us: "Come quickly, my mother is going to talk to you; come quickly, she might be going to die." She took us, in haste, to a house all painted in blue that she opened with a large key. We took off our shoes and found ourselves at the bedside of a very old lady, surrounded by pictures of her childhood and adolescence. Her life seemed to be hanging by a thread. It was as though she had been waiting for us, so that she could finally speak before departing. We set up our cameras, embarrassed about intruding on the privacy of a dying person. Her daughter, conscious of our hesitation, turned toward me: "It's important, my mother wants this to be known!" The old lady herself, barely able to lift her head from her pillow, murmured that she didn't know any more, that she couldn't go on. Her daughter violently tore down the photos of her mother from the walls, one after the other. She brandished them before her eyes, begging: "Mama, Mama, remember, remember!" The mother and daughter, in tears, remembered and recounted.

They had hid a Jewish adolescent in the house, for weeks. The entire Jewish community of the village had already been shot. But this girl could no longer bear to be shut in and one day she went to play in the yard, in front of the door to the house. Germans had come down the street, seen that the girl was Jewish, and shot her against the door.

The dying mother, weeping, fell silent, as though delivered. Her daughter said to us: "Mama wanted that to be known before she died. For us, it was a great trauma that that young girl whom we hid was assassinated so savagely against the front door to our house." I left them, reflecting on the limitless barbarity that all these people had undergone. Every street and house was wounded, bleeding, and blood-stained.

The Holocaust by bullets also included these women and these men who hid, going out only to beg food in the villages. And then one day a denunciation or a German passing by, and they were assassinated. Killing a Jew was an insignificant, legitimate, authorized, and encouraged act that conformed with the directives of the Reich. Protecting a Jew led to capital punishment.

In the village of Chernovo in Crimea we met Vladimir Chtchechro. He had tried to help a young Jewish woman escape. The Jews had been shut into a primary school and were to be taken in a truck to the place of execution. A young Jewish girl, realizing that her death was imminent, jumped from the truck and began running in a last, instinctive bid for survival. Without hesitation, a German seized his Mauser rifle, aimed, shot, and wounded her in the hand. Two of her fingers were torn off. Vladimir told us that he had begged the driver to start the engine and leave her. But the girl, lying on the dirt road, caught hold of a piece of her coat with her good hand to hide her face. "What misfortune!" cried Vladimir, as if he had gone back in time 60 years, and could still save her. The Germans had thought she was dead but when they saw her move, they immediately realized she was still alive. One of them had quickly jumped down from the truck and gone up to her. Terrified, the young girl protected her face even more with her coat. He then smashed her head with the butt of his rifle, thereby killing her. The other Jews watched the scene, terrified. The assassin went to find a peasant with a wheelbarrow or a cart to ask him to take the body and throw it in a well. A farmer in the village named Zedinski was requisitioned for the task. He brought his cart, put a dried cow hide over the bottom of it, placed the body of the wretched girl on it, and took her to the village of Daman,[1] a kilometer and a half from the place of the assassination, to throw her body down a well.

Everyday horror, the unforgiving Shoah, without pity or reason. How many times Vladimir repeated: "If only she had managed not to move, she would have been saved, for everyone thought she was dead."

The rescuers were numerous and discreet.[2] I remember the story of that Ukrainian grandmother who had accompanied her Jewish daughter-in-law Tsilya Meerovna to Babi Yar, thinking the family was going to be deported and she was going to look after her granddaughter Raissa, then aged three. As they had approached the valley of death, the mother, understanding that the whole family was going to be assassinated, shouted to the Ukrainian grandmother: "Take her, say it's your daughter." So the grandmother took Raissa in her arms and ran toward a Ukrainian policeman, saying to him: "I am not Jewish, I'm Ukrainian." The policeman's only response was to try and hit the child's head with the butt of his gun to kill it. In protecting the infant, the grandmother took the blow on the shoulder and fell under the shock. Seeing her on the ground, a German lifted her up and forced her to return into the crowd of people waiting to be shot. The grandmother, crazed with rage and pain, began running with the child in the opposite direction. Gun shots were fired in her direction but she managed to reach the Jewish cemetery, not far from the execution site, without being wounded. She ran between the tombs, for fear that she was being followed, then hid with the little girl behind a tombstone until night fell.

She hid the child for many months. Raissa eventually became a dancer with the opera ballet. It was Raissa who, at Babi Yar, all dressed in red, her eyes hidden behind large sunglasses and holding her own granddaughter by the hand, had talked to us. She came to Babi Yar to to tell us that tale of survival from horror.

I also remember a tiny little lady, with white hair done up in a chignon and the yellow flowery blouse often seen in Galicia. She was called Olga Kokodishka. She was standing very upright on her front steps, her forehead lifted like a resistance fighter who had a score to settle with life. She had lived in Novy Yaritchev during the war. Her family hid Jews in the house. One day, a neighbor had denounced them. The Gestapo arrived at the door of the house and screamed: "You are hiding Jews!" The Germans searched the house from top to bottom, smashing everything on their way. But the Jews had got out of a window at the back. When they realized there were no Jews in the house, they gathered the family outside, on the front steps, and said to them: "You are lucky, they've already left. We haven't found anyone so we will kill only your father." And in front of the whole family they shot the father. At the memory, his daughter Olga, 75, tightened her fists, with rage in her stomach and tears in her eyes: "That is how I lost my father." One saw in her eyes the resentment of someone who has experienced the worst of injustices. And that was how a German, who was just passing through the place and who believed he was saving the world and building an Aryan Europe, destroyed a family because they did not find any Jews in the house.

Maria Kedrovska, Bobovry Kut, region of Kherson, July 11, 2006
Maria was born to a Russian mother and a Jewish father. During the war, she was taken to the edge of a well, where all the Jews were shot or thrown in alive, but was spared that fate. She recounts the unimaginable, a child seeing her whole community being executed.

Patrick Desbois: Were there a lot of Jews in Bobovry Kut before the war?

Maria Kedrovska: The whole village was Jewish; there were only four Russian families.

P.D.: Was there a synagogue?

M.K.: Yes. After the war, it became an oil factory. Today the building is in ruins.

P.D.: What happened when the Germans arrived in Bobovry Kut?

M.K: When they arrived, they assembled all the Jews in the canteen next to the synagogue. Some of those who knew what was to happen left and those who knew nothing stayed—perhaps they knew but they had nowhere to go, or perhaps they didn't want to leave their house. So they were gathered in a stable next to the synagogue; there were seven buildings. They barricaded them and took the Jews there, with dogs, and squeezed them all in. Then they executed them all together.

P.D.: How did they assemble them in the canteen? How did they go to get them?

M.K.: They went to get them from their houses. There was the police and the Germans. They guarded them with dogs. At first, they didn't touch me because they had been told my mother was Russian, and my Jewish father was at the front. Then, they took us anyway, with another woman and her two boys, and they shut us in a cellar.

P.D.: Who shut you in? The Germans?

M.K.: It was a German. We stayed there for three days; they must certainly have been waiting to know what they should do with us. Then a German arrived with a horse and a cart. He was very handsome, and the horse, too, I can still see them. He put the woman and her two boys on the cart and left me and my mother in the cellar. They took us out two hours later. We were walking behind the columns that they were taking to the well. There were a lot of people, I don't know how many; I was small at the time.

P.D.: Did they have the list of people when they arrested them?

M.K.: They simply went from house to house. They were destroying and burning everything. They gathered masses and masses of people, then they took them into the steppe where there was a well. Since the war there has been a monument there on which it is written how many people died. So they put us in the line of people where there was my mother, my father's mother, his two sisters with two children. They were holding my hand and that was how we were taken to the well. Then, at the well, people were killed and thrown in while others threw themselves into it alive.

P.D.: Was the well very deep?

M.K.: Yes, it was one of those wells from which horses drew water. It must have been around 80 meters deep.

P.D.: Did you see members of your family being killed at that time?

M.K.: So we were standing not far from the well. A man in a German uniform took me by the hand, led me to the side of the Germans and they all spoke in German. I don't know how long I stayed there, perhaps an hour, perhaps two. Then, a man came and gave a piece of paper to that German, and after reading it, he took me to another village where I joined two of my cousins. I don't know what was written on the paper. I was small, I was no more than five years old. My cousins were crying. The German then said to us: "Children, don't go to Bobovry Kut, or else they will kill you." Then they hid me and gave me the name Proskoudina.

P.D.: Was all your family killed?

M.K.: Yes. All those who were down there were thrown into the well. I survived by a miracle, thanks to that German. I don't know who he was, perhaps he was an interpreter because he spoke German to the soldiers but Russian to me. In 1949, when I was older and I understood things better, I wanted to know what my real surname was and where my father was.

P.D.: Were you with your mother when you were near the well?

M.K.: No, my mother was thrown out of the line before we got to the well. It seems that she went mad and they put her in prison. I never saw her again.

P.D.: When they took you out of the houses, did they tell you where they were taking you?

M.K.: People knew, of course, that they were going to be killed. There was shouting. They loaded the people in herds, like cattle.

P.D.: Who led you to the well? A policeman, a German?

M.K.: I remember only the Germans, with machine guns and dogs, hitting people with their weapons.

P.D.: Was the well surrounded by soldiers?

M.K.: Yes. There was a team of people who were working for the Germans but they didn't let them get too near the well.

P.D.: How long did the shooting last?

M.K.: Around two hours. Some people fell into the well alive. Shouts were heard for three days.

P.D.: Where did you hide afterwards?

M.K: They took me to another village where my mother's sister-in-law lived with my cousins. My mother's brother was at the front. One day a German came to my aunt's and told her that if they found someone they would kill the whole family. So then they put me in an orphanage in Kalinine.

P.D.: Were you arrested at the same time as everyone else?

M.K.: Yes.

P.D.: Did they give you food to eat when you were shut into the cave?

M.K.: No. I was crying so much, I was hungry. I tried to breastfeed from my mother. But she didn't have any more milk. When I was in the orphanage, all the children had trachoma. They say it was because of the Germans. So they took us all to the regional hospital in Kherson.

P.D.: The Germans never found you again?

M.K.: No.

P.D.: Thank you very much. Do you agree to your testimony being placed in archives and museums?

M.K.: Yes.

XIX

EVERYDAY EVIL

In the village of Strusiv, we were told that the Nazis had staged a kind of *Pessah* in reverse. One evening, the Germans asked the Christians to hang a large cross on the door of their house. The peasants followed this order by taking down the cross from their dining room and fixing it to the outside door. Early the next morning, the Germans arrived in the village and smashed down the door of the houses where there was no cross, went in and shot the inhabitants. They had quickly been able to identify the houses of the Jews.

One evening we met an elderly gentleman of Polish origin who was not very keen to talk. He addressed us briefly, from across the gate without opening it. He was making his way inside when he suddenly turned around and came back toward us: "I must tell you the truth!" This elderly gentleman explained to us how he had hung a cross on his door in the evening. The following day, he realized why he had been asked to do it. He also told us that he got on very well with the Jewish neighbors opposite. "There are still survivors. You can go and question them." We went to the house opposite, less than 10 meters away, from which emerged two brothers, Jews, in their sixties. They told us that their family—their parents and grand-parents—were assassinated in the house by the Germans, because that morning they hadn't had a cross fixed to their door.

Sixty years later, the Christian Yossep Rechilo and the Jew Yakiv Guller, face to face, recounted how one of them had been indirectly associated with a crime of which he had known nothing and the other had his life destroyed by the lack of a cross.

That night in the little town of Strusiv, in the region of Ternopil in Galicia, the Reich perverted the text of the Bible against the Jews.

One day I noticed on a map a village with a name that disturbed me: Sataniv. I asked one of our interpreters if this name was connected with Satan. He said yes, without giving any more details. I asked the team to make a detour. We climbed up to a plateau from which we saw the whole town of Sataniv. Numerous Jewish graves were still there and, in the middle, an inscription on a cement plaque that read: "Here are buried the Jews of Sataniv." How could they have buried all the Jewish victims of that town in a tomb measuring one meter by two meters? In 1939, the Jews represented 48 percent of the population.

I came out of the cemetery feeling rather weary. Weary of the stories that were not exactly true, weary of meeting people who said they wanted to tell us all but who didn't want us to know everything.

In the distance we caught sight of two women. Dressed in shabby coats that protected them from the rain, they were leaning painfully on sticks. They were tending two cows, each attached to a rope. I went to talk to them: "What happened during the war?" They replied, lifting their hands to the sky: "The Jews . . . the Jews . . . They were walled up. They were walled up under the marketplace in a cellar." The Germans had burnt some straw to make smoke and smother them. Then, after closing the door, they had piled two meters of earth on top. The women told us that, for four days afterwards, the Jews had tried to get out, and that one could see the ground of the marketplace moving. On the fifth day, the silence was total. The story stunned me; I had never heard anything like it. How far could people go in terms of sadism, evil, and negating others? It was an example of a limitless imagination in service of destruction. I ventured to ask: "When did you reopen the cellar?"

"In 1954," one of them replied. I couldn't take any more. I turned off the camera and stopped the interview. These people went into the cellar in 1942 and the door wasn't opened until 12 years later!

Sataniv, the town of immurement. In this town, the Germans did not shoot people. They decided to proceed differently, as an example, from lack of time, or through the evil genius of the squadron leader. In this town there were large cellars under the central market that housed small shops, or rather stalls, around a dilapidated building: the former synagogue. They were called the Turkish cellars.

On my return to Washington, I discovered in the Soviet archives that this immurement, carried out by the Ukrainian police, took place on May 15, 1942. According to these archives, the smoke asphyxiated the imprisoned. The Ukrainian witnesses state that the ground moved for four days.

In the village of Bertniki, where the houses are all arranged on the side of a street 200 meters long, no Jews were officially executed. There is no trace of this having occurred, in either the German or Soviet archives. We parked near the first house. Two people were sitting on a bench: a woman, dressed in black, her emaciated face a little rigid, and a man, wearing the brown jacket that is typical in the former socialist republics, who became visibly agitated when his wife wanted to talk to us. She was beginning to say: "This is how it happened . . ."when he cried: "Be quiet! Don't talk to strangers. Be quiet!" At the same moment, a girl came out of the house and made toward them, in the courtyard: "Yes, yes, you have to talk!" The woman sat down again, mute, withdrawn, obeying her husband's injunction. We knew that when people refused to speak, it meant that something serious had happened. So we decided to knock on every door in the street. Each time, an elderly person came out as far as the gate, leaning on a stick. Each one was older than the next, and they invariably replied, with a large smile: "Nothing happened. There were no Jews during the war. There were no executions. There were never any communal graves."

As we went on, we saw all these people staying in the street, watching us go to their neighbors. After 20 houses, 20 elderly people were standing outside in the street, leaning on their sticks. The atmosphere was strange, each one spying on the other to see whether he or she was going to talk. We finally got to the last house. A very beautiful house. After it, there was no more asphalt, just an immense quarry and a magnificent, dense, green forest. In front, an elderly gentleman, rather well dressed, seemed to be watching me. I went up to him. As with the others, I asked if he was there during the war. He replied that he was only 60 years old. He left again without saying a word, closed the gate, and went back inside. Taken aback, I said out loud: "He is the youngest old person I have ever met." I realized that all the signs were telling us that something was going on. I determined not to leave this village without knowing what happened.

We turned around to question all the people on the left side of the street, house after house. Those whom we had questioned on the way up were still standing immobile in front of each house on the right. They were all watching our every move, in silence. No one wanted to speak. After having knocked in vain at all the doors, we went back to the couple. He, very agitated, dragged his wife over to us by the arm and began shouting: "We are going to tell the truth. You see the house down there on the left, the modern house. Well, down there he hid Jews during the war. He hid a lot. And each time he killed them during the night. He smothered them with quilts. When they were dead, he stripped them and took their bodies to the quarry to get rid of them."

We could barely believe our ears. The scene was extremely violent. The man also told us that his wife had been raped. He exhibited her to us, repeating that she had been raped. She remained silent, alone and sad, nodding her head. We left the village, feeling exhausted and re-volted. I will never forget that little village where people saw families, refugees for one night, being asphyxiated, completing the extermina-tion process put in place by the Reich.

The Holocaust by smothering. This was far removed from the cen-tralization of the Shoah, its industrial, modern character. In Ukraine it took on the quality of carnage. People could be shot in a marketplace, beside a cliff as in Yalto, walled up alive as in Sataniv, or else smothered with cushions at night.

Tamara Lopatina, Feodosia, region of Crimea, December 25, 2004
Tamara lives in Feodosia, a pretty Crimean town not far from the sea. In Feodosia there were Jews, but also Krymchaks and Karaites.[1] The

Krymchaks spoke Judeo-Tatar. They did not come the day the Jews were executed, but were summoned a month later, after Himmler decided they were also Jews. Tamara accompanied her friend to the summons, and she was imprisoned with her. A German asked her who she was, and she explained that she was not Jewish, at which they threw her out. She therefore had to abandon her friend and the others. We later found the communal graves of the Krymchaks.

Patrick Desbois: What year were you born?

Tamara Lopatina: 1927.

P.D.: Where did you live before the war?

T.L.: I was born, grew up, and lived here in Feodosia until the war. Afterwards I was sent to Germany.

P.D.: Was there a large Jewish community here?

T.L.: You know, we didn't live apart from each other, we all lived together—the Krymchaks, the Karaites, the Jews, and the Tatars. We were all part of Russia.

P.D.: Do you remember the day the Germans came to the town?

T.L.: They arrived in 1942, I think. Two days after the beginning of the war, planes began bombing our port. Then, nothing happened until the Germans arrived. I was going to school; I was 14 at the time. The day the Germans arrived, I had to go to the prison camp. There was German and Soviet bombing.

P.D.: What happened to the Jews?

T.L.: I don't know. Notices announced that the Jews had to go to the prison with enough food for three days because they were being taken to Palestine. Before that, they had to wear a star.

P.D.: Did they go?

T.L.: Yes, they all went. They received the order in the morning, I don't remember what time, and they went; trucks took them. We were forbidden from going near the prison. Then the Krymchaks received the same order: gather at the prison with provisions before being deported somewhere. But, of course, they knew that they were in fact going to be killed.

P.D.: **Was the prison outside the town?**

T.L.: No, it was in the town beside the marketplace. I accompanied a Krymchak friend there. We had known each other for a long time. At the entrance, a Russian policeman pushed me into the prison and I found myself inside; I was crying. Suddenly a German on a motorbike came up to me and asked me why I was crying. I told him that I was Russian and then he kicked me, and I flew five meters through the air. He told me to leave. He saved me.

P.D.: **Did the Krymchaks also have a yellow star?**

T.L.: No. It happened very quickly for the Krymchaks. They announced that all the Krymchaks had to assemble and they killed them.

P.D.: **You never saw your Krymchak friend again?**

T.L.: No, she was killed with all the other Krymchaks, in a ravine outside the town.

P.D.: **Did people hide so as not to go to the prison?**

T.L.: No, they all went. We wanted to hide my friend but her parents refused, they wanted the whole family to stay together.

P.D.: **Did you go to the execution site after the war?**

T.L.: I have never been there. It is outside the town in the anti-tank ditches. There is a memorial. That is where they shot them. Before shooting them, they made them undress, took their clothes, and their valuable possessions. The earth moved for three days because people were still alive.

P.D.: Do you understand why the Germans killed the Jews and the Krymchaks?

T.L.: I don't know. It was the authorities that decided, we didn't know anything about it. We were also deported, to not far from Breslav. I went in 1943 and came back in 1945. First they sent my sister in 1942, then me in 1943.

P.D.: Do you want to add something?

T.L.: All we ask is to finish our lives well, so that our grandchildren will live well.

XX

IN MEMORY OF DORA

Dora was a little girl who lived in Simferopol in Crimea. She was Krymchak. Dora died at the age of four and a half, assassinated.

In their extermination of the Jews, the Germans first summoned the Asheknazis and then assassinated them. Several months later, they received the order from Himmler to kill the Krymchaks. They answered the summons, were brought in trucks to the extermination site, to "Kilometer Eleven," and were executed one after the other.

Dora was taken off with two other members of her family. Those who had escaped the raid begged two neighbors to go to the extermination site to try to negotiate with the Germans for her not to be killed. When the neighbors arrived at "Kilometer Eleven," they found that the Germans had put up a road block. Traffic was stopped during the shootings. Only the trucks filled with Jews were authorized to pass. On the other side of the barricade, they caught sight of little Dora. She was naked. In the icy cold, she was begging the Germans to give her back her coat: "Give me my jacket, I'll give you my shoes in exchange!" But the Germans listened to no one's requests. Dora was shot.

Many years later, we entered the little museum of the Krymchaks, several rooms in a poor district of Simferopol. A little lady, Nina Dakchi, Dora's half-sister—Dora's father remarried after the war—welcomed us and showed us all the traditional Krymchak costumes. Before leaving, she looked in a cupboard and brought out a little item of clothing in a plastic bag. She held it out to us, saying: "This is Dora's dress, it's the dress of my little sister of four and a half. The Germans took everything from the house but they left the children's clothes, perhaps because they forgot, or because they had scarcely any value. So we kept Dora's clothes and when I was born, I was dressed in them. Here is one of her dresses, the dress she wore before being executed." She added in a very solemn voice: "Put it in a museum."

Little Dora's dress is one of the most poignant elements of this Shoah that left only a few sparse clothes, of no value, after having exterminated a whole population, even children, even tiny children.

September 5, 2007, 10.30 A.M., Paris
Sitting at my desk of dark wood, I hear the fax in the central corridor spluttering into life. My associate Marco Gonzalez hands me a fax on which I see the translation of a Soviet archive.[1] I hold my breath. It is the declaration of Stepan Pelip, forest guard of the immense forest between Poland and Ukraine where 10,000 Jews were executed.

During the German occupation of Rawa-Ruska, I worked as a forester in sections no. 51 and 52 of the forest. That is where the Germans executed the Jewish population. From December 5 to December 12, 1942, the Germans began taking the Jews from the camp to sections no. 51 and 52 of the forest which were surrounded by two hills. This is where the executions took place. My work station was 700 meters from the execution site and so I could see the execution of the Jewish population by the German fascist oppressors.

In November, in that part, French prisoners of war had dug a ditch 18 meters long, 8 meters wide, and nearly 4 meters deep. Very early in the morning of December 5, 1942, seven trucks arrived in the forest. The German gendarmes organized the Jews in groups of six people, no matter what their sex or age and took them to the edge of the pit where there were six Germans with machine guns. As soon as the Jews approached the pit, each gunman shot a person, who fell into the ditch. Then the following six Jews were taken to the edge of the pit. The Germans did not shoot children of less than two or three but threw them alive into the pits where they were covered by the bodies of those who had been shot. I personally saw the Germans tearing babies from their mothers who were at the edge of the pit just before being shot. I saw 30 or so cases like that.

I feel a little faint. Seven years after having rediscovered Rawa-Ruska, camp 325 and the communal graves of the Jews, Rawa-Ruska was again rising to the surface. Was it possible? Did the Nazis requisition French prisoners to dig a pit 18 meters long, the biggest mass grave of Rawa-Ruska? French prisoners. Prisoners from my grandfather's camp. I cannot stop myself thinking about him, he who had led me to trace the Holocaust by bullets, the Jews assassinated by the Nazis, and the forgotten mass graves. Unable to tear my eyes from the testimony of Stepan Pelip, a question will not leave me alone: Did he see it?

ACKNOWLEDGMENTS

I owe what I was able to do and hear in the little villages of Ukraine to so many people that it would need a whole book to record their names.

First of all, thanks to my grandfather, Claudius Desbois, who gave me the thirst for truth. Thank you to my father and mother who gave me the taste for justice and truth.

Thank you to Cardinal Lustiger, who telephoned me after each trip to ask about the research, the discoveries, and how my team was.

Thank you to Monseigneur Vingt-Trois, archbishop of Paris. Thank you to Cardinal Ricard, archbishop of Bordeaux.

Thank you to Mme. Simone Veil, who was president of the Foundation for the Memory of the Shoah. She was the first to speak publicly of my work, in simple, just, and true words. Thank you to the Foundation for the Memory of the Shoah who supported all this research. Without the financial aid, friendship, and the discernment it gave me, I would never have succeeded. Thank you to Mr. Revcolevschi, director of that foundation, who came with us to Ukraine for several days to understand our work, and also to trace a family who had disappeared.

Thank you to Serge and Beate Klarsfeld.

Thank you to Jacky Fredj, Sophie Nagiscarde, and the Center for Contemporary Jewish Documentation which exhibited my work.

Thank you to Paul A. Shapiro, director of the Center for Advanced Holocaust Studies at the United States Holocaust Memorial Museum and to the Museum's director Sarah Bloomfield who gave me access to the center's Soviet archives.

Thank you to the archive of Ludwigsburg, the central judiciary office of the Länder which gave access to the German archives. Thank you to the Targum Shlishi Foundation.

Thank you to the Victor Pinchuk Foundation, the Claims Conference, and the Task Force. Thank you to the World Jewish Congress, to Maram Stern, and Serge Cwajenbaum.

Thank you to Dr. Richard Prasquier, president of the Representative Council of the Jewish Institutions of France; thank you to Marcello Pezzetti, director of the Shoah Museum of Milan; thank you to Israel Singer, who was the first to believe in the relevance of our work.

Thank you also to the historians Édouard Husson, Martin Dean, and Dieter Pohl for their valuable help.

Thank you to the rabbinical authorities, Rabbi Yacov Blaich of Kiev, Rabbi Kaminezki of Dnipropretosk, and Rabbi Schlessinger of London.

But above all a big thank you to all those who contributed to the research in Ukraine, particularly as it was often carried on when it was raining and cold: Svetlana Biryulova (interpretation and research of witnesses); Guillaume Ribot (photography and coordination of work); Andrej Umanksy (translation and research in the archives); Mikhailo "Micha" Strutinsky (ballistics expert); Pierre-Philippe Preux (script writing); Patrice Bensimon (translation into Ukrainian and French); Thierry Soval (camera); Pierre-Jérôme Biscarat; Yaroslav Nadyak (former deputy mayor of Rawa-Ruska); Vera Savchak (translation); Jean-François Bodin (notes); Victor Fleury (notes); Henri Planet (script);

ACKNOWLEDGMENTS

Emmanuel Salunier, Béchir Chemsa, Alain Durand (camera); Roger Garnier, Eric Pellet (camera); Andrej Demtchouk (translation); Galina, Eugenia Pace; David Baisnenou, Mona Oren, Bogdan Gorayetsky, Eugenia, Ivan, Bruno Moreira, Vassili Vakhnyanki, Vassili, Vitaly (transport); Yael Halberthal, Taras Yatsoulak (lawyers); Françoise Planet, Michel Roux (accounting). A big thank you to the mayors and the administration of the little towns of Ukraine, to the shopkeepers of the shops, and to the priests of the Ukrainian parishes. And also thank you, in France, to Marco Gonzalez, coordinator of Yahad, Séverin Mélès, and Jacqueline Séïtè.

Thank you to Sophie Charnavel and Virginie Fuertes.

And thank you to the thousands of Ukrainian men and women who took the risk, on a little wooden bench, of revealing the truth.

Royalties from the sale of this book will be given to the Yahad-In-Unum organization.

YAHAD-IN-UNUM

Yahad-In-Unum is a joint initiative for human dignity, dialogue, and solidarity.

Yahad-In-Unum was created in January 2004 on the initiative of Cardinal Jean-Marie Lustiger, then archbishop of Paris, with Cardinal Philippe Barbarin, archbishop of Lyon, Cardinal Jean-Pierre Ricard, archbishop of Bordeaux, Rabbi Israel Singer, former president of the World Jewish Congress, and of Mr. Serge Cwajgenbaum, secretary-general of the World Jewish Congress and Mr. Pinchas Shapiro, with the objective of deepening knowledge and cooperation between Catholics and Jews.

To express the aspirations of the project, the association took the name of Yahad-In-Unum, *yahad* and *in unum* both meaning "together" in Hebrew and in Latin.

Yahad-In-Unum illustrates and concretizes the considerable evolution of relations between Christians and Jews during the previous half-century.

The work of the Vatican II council and the words and actions of Pope John Paul II, pursued by Benedict XVI, have definitively changed the issues and created the conditions for a mutual loyal and warm trust. The collapse of the Soviet regime, almost half a century after that of the Nazi regime, has opened new perspectives to both Christianity and

Judaism in Europe. In 2004 and 2005, the most renowned representatives of Jewish orthodoxy entered into an essentially religious dialogue with Catholic bishops in an atmosphere of mutual respect of differences. Jews and Christians live in societies marked by a strong secularism. Each of them, conscious of an ethic and a responsibility received on Mount Sinai by the giving of the Law, are finding the need not only for a dialog but also for a religious fraternity geared toward service of society.

Yahad-In-Unum has a two-fold aim: To support initiatives of dialog between Catholic and Jewish religious authorities; and to respond to the great needs of the today's world through common projects based on an ethic inspired by the Law received on Mount Sinai.

NOTES

FOREWORD

1. Archbishop of Paris Jean-Marie Cardinal Lustiger, now deceased, and Andre Cardinal Vingt-Trois, who succeeded him, have both provided strong backing. Both visited the United States Holocaust Memorial Museum, in 2006 and 2008 respectively, for the purpose of speaking publicly about the imperative of Holocaust education and the importance of cooperative work by Christians and Jews to study the Holocaust.

2. The full extent of these collections can be explored through the regularly-updated *Archival Guide to the Collections of the United States Holocaust Memorial Museum,* located on the Museum's web site at www.ushmm.org.

3. On January 2, 2008, Yahad-In Unum, University of Paris IV-Sorbonne, and the United States Holocaust Memorial Museum signed an agreement to jointly foster new research and expanded teaching about the Holocaust, with special focus on the Holocaust in the east. The three organizations and the *Memorial de la Shoah* co-sponsored an international conference on the Holocaust in Ukraine in Paris in October 2007.

PREFACE

1. A *kolkhoz* was an agricultural co-operative in the Soviet Union that replaced the *artels,* the associations of craftsmen and other workers. The word is a contraction of the Russian for "collective economy." The *kolkhozes* were established by Joseph Stalin after the abolition of private agricultural estates in 1928 and their conversion to collectives. The *kolkhozes* started being privatised in 1992, in a process that was completed after the fall of the Soviet Union.

2. The Ukrainian Insurgent Army (UPA) was created on October 14, 1942 by the "B wing" of the Organization of Ukrainian Nationalists (OUN), and led by Stepan Bandera (1909–1959). Banned by the German forces, this paramilitary organization conducted actions against the German Administration in the Ukrainian district of Galicia and in the Ukraine *Reichskommissariat,* as well as military actions against the Soviet partisans and the Armia Krajowa (the Polish Resistance Movement). UPA finally conducted a "purification policy" of western Ukraine which caused the death of tens of thousands of Poles in the districts of Volhynia and Galicia. After the war, UPA's main enemy were the Soviet security services which ceased to exist only at the end of the 1960s. Soviet forces killed at least 50,000 Bandera supporters, and deported to Siberia double that number. Some of the victims were only civilians who had helped or hidden Bandera

supporters. Stepan Bandera himself was arrested in Lviv by German troops on June 30, 1941 during a declaration of an independent Ukrainian state. He was then imprisoned in the Sachsenhausen German concentration camp until 1944. After his liberation, he was sentenced in absentia by a Soviet tribunal, and took refuge in Germany. In 1959 he was assassinated in Munich by order of the KGB.

CHAPTER 3

1. Shawl worn by Jews during prayer.
2. Or phylactery; small leather box containing prayers taken from the Torah. Men wear them on the head and arm when praying.
3. Grand Rabbi of the Synagogue de la Victoire in Paris and vice president of Judeo-Christian Friendship in France.
4. Yad Vashem is the Israeli national Halocaust memorial erected on Mount Herzl in Jerusalem. It was consecrated to the six million Jews who died during the Holocaust. "Even unto them will I give in mine house and within my walls a place and a name better than of sons and of daughters: I will give them an everlasting name, that shall not be cut off." Isaiah 56.5
5. Operation Reinhardt was the code name given to the extermination campaign that took place in the camps of Sobibor, Belzec, and Treblinka on Polish territory, between July 1942 and October 1943, and in which nearly two million Jews and 50,000 Romanies (known as Gypsies) were killed.
6. "Intervention Group." Four *Einsatzgruppen* had been created with the specific purpose of acting inside USSR territory, and each was assigned a region: *Einsatzgruppe* A (Baltic States and part of Russia), *Einsatzgruppe* B (Belarus and part of Russia), *Einsatzgruppe* C (part of Ukraine and part of Russia), and *Einsatzgruppe* D (Bessarabia, part of Ukraine, Crimea, and the Caucasus). These *Einsatzgruppen* were subdivided into *Einsatzkommandos* and *Sonderkommandos,* veritable mobile killing machines that acted independently from each other. They had one mission: to exterminate the Jews, Romanies, and the mentally handicapped, and to kill political commissioners.
7. As head of the regional militia in Lyon during the German occupation, Paul Touvier took part in the persecution of Jews and resistance fighters. He was condemned to death in absentia by the courts of Lyon and Chambéry in 1946 and 1947, pardoned in 1971 by President Georges Pompidou, and finally condemned to life imprisonment in 1994 for crimes against humanity. He died in Fresnes in prison in 1996.
8. Marc Aron is president of the *Conseil Représentatif des Institutions juives de France* (CRIF; Representative Council for Jewish Institutions in France), and of B'naï B'rith. Alain Jakubowicz is a lawyer (Lyon bar) and former president of CRIF for the Rhône-Alpes region in France.

CHAPTER 4

1. Italian researcher, director of the audio-visual department at the Center of Contemporary Jewish Documentation in Milan.
2. A former goods station and point of arrival of the deportees to Auschwitz until spring 1944. Here the convoys stopped, and the deportees were separated into two queues directly on the platform: one destined to Auschwitz I, straight for the gas chambers, and the other to Auschwitz II-Birkenau for forced labor. The deportees

had to walk off the platform to the camps. The platform was eventually lengthened to reach inside Birkenau.

CHAPTER 5

1. The official name was Stalag 325, created in spring 1942 by the Germans as a reprisal camp for French and Belgian prisoners of war who had tried to escape from another camp or who did not want to work. The number of prisoners at Rawa-Ruska and its sub-camps increased steadily until it reached 24,000 by January 19, 1943, when it was closed and the prisoners were transferred to other camps.

2. "In Rawa-Ruska camp where I was, the regime and the conditions were atrocious. The prisoners of war (POWs) were shut up in shacks; in winter, the Germans would deliberately leave the doors and windows open the whole day so that people inside would freeze to death. We were given barely any food, and prisoners cut up the corpses of POWs who had died of hunger and cooked that human flesh. The Germans saw all this and jeered at it. With my own eyes, I saw the flesh of a dozen prisoners of war being cooked. Shootings and blows took 150 to 200 men a day. The bodies of POWs were taken in tractor trailers into the forest of Wadowice where they were thrown into a pit specially dug by the prisoners themselves." Report from the district Soviet commission established to enquire into the crimes of the fascist German invaders, committed in the district of Rawa-Ruska, dated September 24–30, 1944

3. *La Région de Lviv pendant la grande guerre patriotique 1941–1945*, edited by the archive of the Communist party of Ukraine in the region of Lviv, Kameniar, 1968.

4. The Soviet commissions of inquiry were created to evaluate the war crimes perpetrated by the Germans with a view to their compensation. These commissions very often opened the mass graves.

5. Camp of Jewish workers.

CHAPTER 6

1. This museum exhibits works by W. Wathel, M. Gottlib, L. Wein, O. Dobrovolski, S. Merkel, J. Stik, and E. Kunke.

2. Guillaume Ribot, *Chaque printemps les arbres fleurissent à Auschwitz*, Grenoble: Ville de Grenoble, 2005.

3. *Camps en France*, in partnership with the Foundation for the Memory of the Deportation, April 2008.

4. Ninety Jewish children were executed in August 1941 under the orders of *SS-Standartenführer* Paul Blobel (see next endnote) and his deputy *SS-Obersturmführer* August Häfner, members of *Sonderkommando* 4a.

5. Paul Blobel, German architect, was responsible as the head of the *Sonderkommando* 4a, for numerous executions in Ukraine, notably the execution of at least 33,371 Jews on September 29 and 30, 1941. After suffering from health problems, he organised in 1942 Operation 1005, which consisted of wiping out all traces of the mass executions committed in the occupied territories

6. The Third Reich and territories annexed by it were divided politically into *Gau* headed by a *Gauletier,* a member of the Nazi party.

7. "I went alone into the woods. The Wehrmacht had already dug a tomb. They brought the children in a trailer pulled by a tractor. I didn't pay attention to the technical procedure. The Ukrainians were waiting, shaking. They brought the children down from

the trailer. They were lined up along the side of the grave so that they would fall inside when they were shot. The Ukrainians did not aim for any particular part of the body. They fell into the pit. Their wimpering was indescribable. I will never forget that scene. I find it very difficult to bear. I often remember a little blonde girl who took hold of my hand. She was also killed, later [. . .] The grave was near a woods. It wasn't near the shooting field. The execution must have taken place around 3:30 or 4 pm [. . .] Many children took four or five bullets before dying." Quoted in Richard Rhodes, *Masters of Death: the SS- Einsatzgruppen and the Invention of the Holocaust,* New York: Alfred A. Knopf, 2002.

CHAPTER 7

1. Words spoken by the head of *Einsatzgruppe* D, the *SS-Gruppenführer* Otto Ohlendorf, who ordered a great number of executions in Moldavia, southern Ukraine and Russia in his conversations with a psychologist during the Nuremberg trial of the *Einsatzgruppen* members.
2. Statement given by Ludwig Maurer, federal archive of Ludwigsburg, Germany, BAL B162/5646 p. 1171.

CHAPTER 8

1. Gerhardt Riegner was the author of the famous telegram sent in August 1942 to Rabbi Stephen Wise in New York. He had received his information on August 1, from Sagalowitz, who had been in touch with a German industrialist who knew about the decision to exterminate the Jews. Here is the text of the telegram: "*Received alarming report that in Fuhrers headquarters plan B discussed and under consideration all Jews in countries occupied or controlled under German number 3 ½ to 4 millions should after deportation and concentration in east at one blow exterminated to resolve once for all Jewish question in Europe.*"
2. Yves Ternon, "La qualité de la preuve" in *CDCA, L'Actualité du génocide des Arméniens,* preface by Jack Lang, Edipol, Paris, 1999.

CHAPTER 10

1. Friedrich Jeckeln was the head of the SS and of the police in the southern region of Russia.
2. Mayor and representative of the state in the administrative areas of western Ukraine before 1939. The German authorities took over the *starosta* system by putting in mayors who were in post before 1939 or new mayors. Their functions were limited and they were under the authority of the German administration. Their involvement in the executions varied in each case but was sometimes an active, willing participation.

CHAPTER 11

1. The "Conference on Jewish Material Claims against Germany." The Claims Conference was founded in 1951 in New York to represent and offer reparations for the victims and the Jewish survivors of the Shoah.
2. A little town in the region of Khmelnitski in Ukraine.
3. After hesitation, the Nazi authorities decided that the Krymchaks belonged to the "Jewish race." A great number of the 5,000 Krymchaks living in Crimea before 1941 were executed.

4. The extermination site is called "Kilometer Eleven" because it is situated exactly 11 kilometers from the town center of Simferopol, near the motorway to Feodosiya (Theodosiya). More than 10,000 Jews were executed there by the units of *Einsatzgruppe* D and the *Feldgendarmerie* between December 9 and 13 1941.

5. A little village on the banks of the Bug river in the region of Nikolayev in Ukraine. More than 50,000 Jews from the area of Odessa and Bessarabia were deported to Bogdanovskoie and crammed into pigsties. Forty thousand Jews were executed by the Ukrainian police, with the help of the Roumanian gendarmerie from December 21 to 23 and 28 to 31. The bodies of the dead were then burnt.

6. The director of the Center of Advanced Holocaust Studies, in the Holocaust Memorial Museum in Washington, D.C.

7. Senior lecturer at the University of La Sorbonne, Paris IV, where he studied the history of Nazism under Ian Kershaw. Having specialized in the history of the Nazi police for several years, he accompanied me several times to Ukraine.

8. The official tasks of the *Feldgendarmerie* (German military police) were various, ranging from regulating traffic to the hunting down of deserters, and also to implementing military occupation of territories under the control of the German army.

9. The *Ordnungspolizei* was created in 1936 by Heinrich Himmler who had the idea of merging the police and the SS. Its principal task was maintaining public order in large towns and villages. It did not deal with major crimes, for that was the task of the *Sicherheitspolizei*. It was composed of several different types of police. Units were transferred from the Reich into the occupied territories to undertake administration; certain units systematically took part in the executions of the local Jewish population. According to the latest historical research, more than 20,000 police participated in the Shoah of the East. It is estimated that more than 2 million Jewish victims were killed with the direct participation of the *Ordnungspolizei*.

10. The western part of Ukraine formed part of the *Generalgouvernement* as the district of "Galicia." The regions of the central part were regrouped into the *Reichskommissariat* of Ukraine. The eastern part and the Crimea were under military administration.

11. In Katyn in spring 1940, the NKVD (the acronym of *Narodnil Kommissariat Vnoutrennikh Diel,* meaning People's Commissariat for Internal Affairs) assassinated several thousand officers and members of the Polish elite. The Nazis tried to use the crime for ideological ends and thereby sow discord between the allies. It was not until 1990 that Gorbatchev's USSR finally admitted that the NKVD was solely responsible for that killing and presented an official apology to Poland.

12. Leon Weliczer Wells, *The Janowska Road* and *The Death Brigade.*

CHAPTER 12

1. The term *Volksdeutscher* (lit: member of the German people) had been used since World War I to designate people who had German as their mother tongue but who lived outside the Reich and had citizenship of another country. Each *Volksdeutsch* had a special identity document and an attestation of racial purity. They had advantages over the local population, with access to special shops and food rations. Sometimes the clothes of executed Jews were distributed to them.

CHAPTER 13

1. Term describing oral law in Judaism.

CHAPTER 14

1. "Red peasant" in Yiddish.
2. *Ortskommandantur* and *Feldkommandantur* were units of the *Wehrmacht* which represented the military administration in the occupied territories. The *Ortskommandantur,* the *Feldkommandantur*—these units were mobile and could accompany the movements of the front.
3. Verkhovna Rada: unicameral parliament of Ukraine.
4. Wooden percussion instrument.

CHAPTER 17

1. "Busk. An isolated village in the far reaches of Galicia, near the border with Russian Poland. All the woods are mud. Leprous houses made of crumbling cob, disjointed planks, tin, and filthy bits of rag. Boggy streets with a log-built road on which the long cart bumps along painfully, repeatedly throwing the hapless traveller back onto the straw. Ducks and geese run chaotically among the comings and goings of the muddy boots from which emerge emaciated Jews, with their piercing eyes and their Talmudic side locks, Ruthens combining abundant hair and coats made of sheep fleeces, Mongols, red-haired, blond or dark Kalmuks . . . Slavs of all origins with their long white smocks and deceptively innocent blue eyes. An Asian encampment suddenly appearing in the mud. And to complete the vision, in the prairie are tents around which slumber a population of semi-naked Bohemians." From Georges Clemenceau, *Au pied du Sinaï,* Paris: Georges Grès et Cie, 1920,
2. Small Ukrainian town near the Polish border with a Jewish community in existence since the fourteenth century. The Hassidic dynasty of Belz was founded by the Rabbi Shalom of Belz.
3. *SS-Untersturmführer* Wilhelm Rebay von Ehrenwiesen was the first of the *Kreishauptmann* (the head of the *Kreis*), followed, in summer 1942 by *SS-Unterstrurmführer* Joachim Nehring. Von Ehrenwiesen was never brought to trial because of insufficient evidence. Nehring had to stand charges before German justice but he was acquitted by the Stade circuit court in 1981.
4. Yiddish term that designates a non-Jewish person who helps a Jewish family during Shabbat by carrying out tasks such as preparing dishes or lighting the fire.
5. The *desiatnik* was a person charged with specific community and public order functions within the soviet local administration. He performed his functions for a cluster of houses (usually ten, hence the name which is derived from the Russian word for "ten"). The *desiatniks* had been kept in place by the German occupiers. Certain tasks of the *desiatnik* during the war were linked to the executions. He often had to store the spades and organize the labor to dig or fill in the pits. His orders, often given under threat of death, came directly from the German authorities or the mayor.
6. "Jewish council." An administrative system put in place by the German authorities after the occupation and the creation of a ghetto. It was the link between the German administration and the Jewish population. It had the functions of providing social aid and supplies to the Jews, and organizing the labor required by the German authorities. At the end of 1941 there were 40 *Judenrat* in Galicia alone. They were

composed of 5 to 12 members; the president was appointed by the Germans, and he then chose the other members. The *Judenrat* was usually made up of important and well-known figures in the village.

7. An identity card. The witness probably had an authorization stamped on his identity card permitting his entry into the ghetto, something not granted generally to the local population.

8. "Protection police" who corresponded to the municipal police responsible for maintaining order. These police were subject to the *Ordnungspolizei,* the regular German police.

9. On May 21, 1943, the ghetto of Busk was liquidated by members of the *Sipo-Außenstelle* of Sokal, the Ukrainian police, and the *Volksdeutche.* One thousand two hundred Jews were executed. Three hundred Jews who were fit for work were transferred to the Yanovska camp in Lviv.

10. Garf, Fonds 7021, Opis 67, and Delo 82; Washington archives RG–22.002M, Reel 13.

11. In June 1990, an Australian team had carried out field work in the village of Serniki in the region of Rovne, at the request of the Australian judicial system. They needed evidence for the case of Ivan Polyukhovich, a former forest worker in the village who had emigrated to Australia, and had been accused of having participated in an execution of over 500 Jews. Polyukhovich was acquitted in 1993 by the Adelaide circuit court.

12. Israeli organization that ensures that the bodies of victims of terrorist attacks are buried according to Jewish law.

13. For instance, on September 21, 1942, the day of Yom Kippur, 600 Jews classed as unfit for work were executed with other Jews near the town of Kamionka-Strumilova.

14. Other Jews were able to escape to the forest but some of them were caught by the Ukrainian police.

15. *Kaddish* means "sanctification" in English. It is a prayer of blessing used during funeral rituals, prayer services and memorial ceremonies.

16. "Magnified and sanctified as the Great Name In the world that He created to His will."

17. The acronym of *Narodnil Kommissariat Vnoutrennikh Diel* ("People's Commissariat for Internal Affairs"). In the ex-USSR, it was the secret police created in 1934 to replace the OGPU, before being re-baptised MVD in 1946.

18. These police, who were armed with batons, had the tasks of guarding the ghettos, arresting people who were to be deported, and collecting money as demanded by the German authorities.

19. Identity card. The local population and also the Jews had to be able to show their identity card during a check. On the Jewish identity cards a large "J" appeared and sometimes a fingerprint. In addition, the card sometimes included information about the person's work status, which could save him or her during a deportation.

CHAPTER 18

1. A village that no longer exists.

2. More than 400 Ukrainians received the medal of the Righteous Among the Nations from the State of Israel for having saved Jews of the Ukraine.

CHAPTER 19

1. The Karaites (Karaim) who lived in Crimea rejected the oral Torah in their religion and did not consider themselves Jewish. In 1939, the German authorities had already decided that the Karaites did not belong to the "Jewish race."

CHAPTER 20

1. GARF, Fonds 7021, Opis 67, Delo 78 (Rawa-Ruska and Gorodok).

INDEX

❶ PRE-WAR JEWISH POPULATION
(by Province in Pre-1941 censuses)

BELARUS

RUSSIA

POLAND

Volyn
>130 000*

Rivne
>110 000*

Zhytomyr
125 007

Chernihiv
31 887

Sumy
16 363

Kiev

Lviv
±380 000*

Khmelnytsky
121 335

Ternopil
±125 000*

Poltava
46 928

Kharkiv
136 746

Luhansk
19 949

297 409**

SLOVAKIA

Ivano-
Frankivsk
±130 000*

Vinnytsia
141 825

Cherkasy

Zakarpattia
±125 000*

Chernivtsi
67 078

Kirovohrad
26 419

Dniepropetrovsk
129 439

Donetsk
65 556

HUNGARY

ROMANIA

MOLDAVIA

Nikolayev
>38 000*

Zaporizhia
<40 000*

Odessa
±270 000*

Kherson
>28 000*

AZOV SEA

0 50 100   200 km

* Population estimated from the
  calculations of Alexandre Krouglov
  (Professor of Social Science, Kharkiv
  State Technical University).

** Combined jewish population of
   Kiev and Chernihiv, which were
   unified in 1954.

Crimea
65 452

BLACK SEA

ROMANIA

© Pierre Gay / Andrej Umansky – Source : KROUGLOV A., *Entsyklopedija Holokosta*, Kiev 2000.

❷ 1941. THE DESTRUCTION OF THE JEWISH
POPULATION (by Province)

BELARUS

RUSSIA

POLAND

Volyn

Rivne

Zhytomyr

Kiev

Chernihiv

Sumy

Lviv

Ternopil

Khmelnytsky

Poltava

Kharkiv

Luhansk

SLOVAKIA

Ivano-
Frankivsk

Zakarpattia

Chernivtsi

Vinnytsia

Cherkasy

Kirovohrad

Dniepropetrovsk

Donetsk

HUNGARY

ROMANIA

MOLDAVIA

Nikolayev

Zaporizhia

Odessa

Kherson

AZOV SEA

0 50 100   200 km

Number of deaths per region:

▓ > 50 000 killed.
▓ 20 000 to 50 000 killed.
▓ 10 000 to 20 000 killed.
▓ 5 000 to 10 000 killed.
░ < 5 000 killed.

BLACK SEA

Crimea

ROMANIA

© Pierre Gay / Andrej Umansky – Source : KROUGLOV A., *Entsyklopedija Holokosta*, Kiev 2000.

❸ 1942. THE DESTRUCTION OF THE JEWISH POPULATION (by Province)

BELARUS

POLAND

Volyn

Rivne

Zhytomyr

Chernihiv

Sumy

RUSSIA

Lviv

Kiev

Ternopil Khmelnytsky

Poltava

Kharkiv

SLOVAKIA

Ivano-
Frankivsk

Luhansk

Zakarpattia

Vinnytsia

Cherkasy

HUNGARY

Chernivtsi

Kirovohrad

Dniépropetrovsk

Donetsk

ROMANIA

MOLDAVIA

Nikolayev

Zaporizhia

0 50 100   200 km

Odessa

Kherson

Number of deaths per region:

AZOV SEA

> 50 000 killed.

20 000 to 50 000 killed.

BLACK SEA

Crimea

10 000 to 20 000 killed.

ROMANIA

5 000 to 10 000 killed.

< 5 000 killed.

© Pierre Gay / Andrej Umansky – Source : KROUGLOV A., *Entsyklopedija Holokosta*, Kiev 2000.

❹ 1943-1944 THE DESTRUCTION OF THE JEWISH POPULATION (by Province)

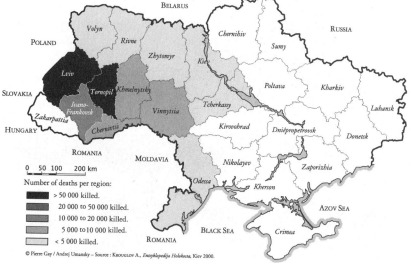

BELARUS

POLAND

Volyn

Rivne

Zhytomyr

Chernihiv

RUSSIA

Sumy

Lviv

Kiev

SLOVAKIA

Ternopil Khmelnytsky

Poltava

Kharkiv

Ivano-
Frankivsk

Zakarpattia

Vinnytsia

Tcherkassy

Luhansk

HUNGARY

Chernivtsi

Kirovohrad

Dniépropetrovsk

Donetsk

ROMANIA

MOLDAVIA

Nikolayev

Zaporizhia

0 50 100   200 km

Odessa

Kherson

Number of deaths per region:

AZOV SEA

> 50 000 killed.

20 000 to 50 000 killed.

10 000 to 20 000 killed.

BLACK SEA

Crimea

5 000 to 10 000 killed.

< 5 000 killed.

ROMANIA

© Pierre Gay / Andrej Umansky – Source : KROUGLOV A., *Entsyklopedija Holokosta*, Kiev 2000.

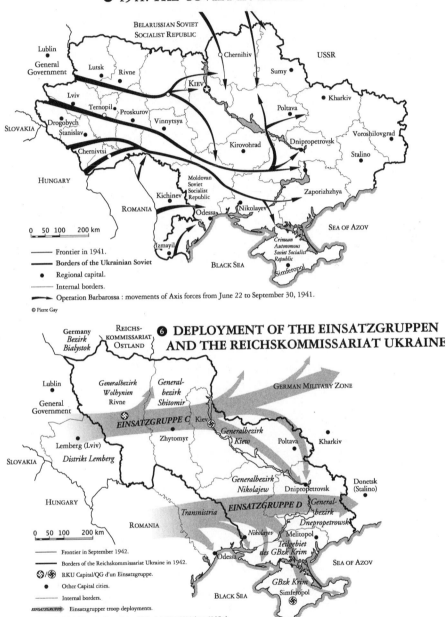

❺ 1941. THE SOVIET INVASION

BELARUSSIAN SOVIET
SOCIALIST REPUBLIC

Lublin

General
Government

Lutsk

Rivne

Chernihiv

KIEV

USSR

Sumy

Kharkiv

Lviv

Ternopil

Proskurov

Vinnytsya

Poltava

SLOVAKIA

Drogobych

Stanislav

Chernivtsi

Kirovohrad

Dnipropetrovsk

Voroshilovgrad

Stalino

HUNGARY

Moldovan
Soviet
Socialist
Republic

Kichinev

ROMANIA

Odessa

Nikolayev

Zaporizhzhya

SEA OF AZOV

0 50 100   200 km

Izmayil

Crimean
Autonomous
Soviet Socialist
Republic

BLACK SEA

Simferopol

——— Frontier in 1941.

▬▬▬ Borders of the Ukrainian Soviet

● Regional capital.

·········· Internal borders.

➤ Operation Barbarossa : movements of Axis forces from June 22 to September 30, 1941.

© Pierre Gay

❻ DEPLOYMENT OF THE EINSATZGRUPPEN AND THE REICHSKOMMISSARIAT UKRAINE

Germany
Bezirk
Bialystok

REICHS-
KOMMISSARIAT
OSTLAND

Lublin

General
Government

Generalbezirk
Wolhynien
Rivne

General-
bezirk
Shitomir

GERMAN MILITARY ZONE

EINSATZGRUPPE C

Kiew

Generalbezirk
Kiew

Poltava

Kharkiv

Lemberg (Lviv)

Distrikt Lemberg

Zhytomyr

SLOVAKIA

HUNGARY

Generalbezirk
Nikolajew

Dnipropetrovsk

Donetsk
(Stalino)

Transnistria

EINSATZGRUPPE D

General-
bezirk
Dnepropetrowsk

ROMANIA

Nikolayev

Melitopol

0 50 100   200 km

Odessa

Teilgebiet
des GBzk Krim

SEA OF AZOV

——— Frontier in September 1942.

▬▬▬ Borders of the Reichskommissariat Ukraine in 1942.

🔯/🔯 RKU Capital/QG d'un Einsatzgruppe.

● Other Capital cities.

·········· Internal borders.

EINSATZGRUPPE Einsatzgrupper troop deployments.

GBzk Krim

Simferopol

BLACK SEA

© Pierre Gay / Andrej Umansky – Source :Belarus National Archive, *391-1-4, page 80*, Minsk.